"Most books are either clear or profound; this is both. Most books are either traditional or up to date; this is both. Most books are either theoretical or practical; this is both. Most books are either complex or simple; this is both. A delight to read—and to live!"

**Dr. Peter Kreeft**
Professor of Philosophy and
Catholic best-selling author

"In a quippy conversational style, laced with wit and wisdom, Jon gives a timely and liberating message—to truly attain happiness we must pursue holiness. This book ignites a passion for embracing the plan of sheer goodness that God has for each of us, a plan that comes with true freedom!"

**Kelly Wahlquist**
Founder of WINE: Women In the
New Evangelization

"Who doesn't want to be free? But what is freedom? With his characteristic wit and wisdom Jon leads us in some rich reflections on some of the men and women who best embody and model freedom: the saints. Thanks, Jon!"

**Fr. John Riccardo**
Author of *Heaven Starts Now*

"Leonetti gets it. *Life, Liberty, and the Pursuit of Holiness* is a refreshing read. I highly recommend it to anyone who wants to recalibrate their worldview!"

**Curtis Martin**
Founder of FOCUS

"Jon Leonetti persuasively demonstrates that true happiness can only be attained through pursuing holiness. His work is like a wrecking ball to the walls that we build around our hearts. If you long to be a saint, this is the next book you should read!"

**DR. RYAN MARR**
Director of the National Institute
for Newman Studies

"Jon Leonetti has a knack for redirecting the fruitless clamor for happiness to a gritty pursuit of holiness. Life, Liberty, and the Pursuit of Holiness is a shot of Catholic motivation that sends you back out into the world, fired up to serve."

**SONJA CORBITT**
Best-selling author of *Fulfilled:
Uncovering the Biblical Foundations
of Catholicism*, Ascension Press

"Wise, practical, and entertaining! Jon's book will show you how to live entirely for Jesus and become a saint!"

**BERT GHEZZI**
Author of *Saints at Heart*

# LIFE, LIBERTY, AND THE PURSUIT OF HOLINESS

# Life, Liberty, *and the* Pursuit *of* Holiness

Jon Leonetti

*To Teresa, Joseph, Gianna, and Anthony*

*I love you*

# Contents

*Prologue*                                     xi

1. God's Gift to the World                      1

2. God's Plan for Your Life                    19

3. So, Why the Catholic Church?                41

4. The Battle for Liberty                      65

5. To Know or to Know About                    81

6. Three Models for Deeper Prayer              93

7. Backyard Missionary                        121

8. Holiness Personified                       139

   *Notes*                                    169

   *Bibliography*                             171

# Prologue

LIFE, LIBERTY, AND THE PURSUIT OF . . . WHAT? I've always heard that as "Life, liberty, and the pursuit of happiness," you say. And you're right, of course. That's the way it is in our Declaration of Independence. "We hold these truths to be self-evident, that all men are created equal, that they are endowed by their Creator with certain unalienable Rights, that among these are Life, Liberty and the pursuit of Happiness." Thomas Jefferson was certainly right about that. In fact, that's the whole point of this little book: God, your Creator, *did* give you life, and he *does* give you liberty, and the only reason for living is to pursue happiness.

So what's with my change to the wording? Well, I'm giving you a little shortcut. You could spend your life pursuing happiness and never catch up to it. The fact is that there's only one way to find happiness, and that's to pursue holiness with everything you've got.

God had a reason for creating you—not just human beings in general, but you in particular. He created you to spend eternity in Heaven with Him. He meant for you to love Him forever, so He could love you forever. But there's a catch. He also gave you freedom. You can make the choice not to love Him. After all, it wouldn't be love if you didn't have a choice. You can't build a machine that has the capacity for authentic love.

So what do we do with our freedom? Well, that's where this book comes in. Americans take their pursuit of happiness very seriously, but the strange thing is that a lot of us don't end up very happy. We chase and chase after happiness, and it always gets away. The reason for that (as you probably knew I was going to tell you) is that we're chasing the wrong things. We run after "stuff." We look for wealth, power, and sex, and we think those things will make us happy. But they won't in and of themselves, because that's not what we're made for. We're made for a much better happiness than those things can ever give you. That's what this book is all about. You could think of it as a self-help book: *Find Your Way to Happiness with These Eight Weird Tricks!* Except that they're not weird at all, because they're the tried-and-true methods the saints have been using for 2000 years. You won't find any trendy psychobabble in this book. Instead, you'll find what we know works to get us moving on the road to Heaven. But that doesn't mean we can't have some fun along the way.

You'll hear some great stories, meet some interesting characters, and maybe laugh a few times if I've done my job right. (Or you'll smile indulgently because you don't want to hurt my feelings, and that's good, too.) Most of all, you'll learn why Christians are really free, even when all the rest of the world is in shackles. And you'll learn what we can do with all that freedom.

It's time to declare your independence from the things that hold you back. It's time to tell Satan he can't boss you around anymore. It's time to get holy, or die trying.

## CHAPTER 1

# God's Gift to the World

YOU ARE GOD'S GIFT TO THE WORLD.
Don't let that go to your head. Remember, I'm the one who wrote a book called *The Art of Getting Over Yourself*. But I do want you to remember that. You are God's gift to the world. God put you here because the world wouldn't be quite right without you.

This is where we Christians have an advantage over a lot of other people. We understand that we're here for a reason. Human life isn't just a random accident, the way some materialists would see it. It's not an endless, painful austerity to be escaped from, the way some Eastern religions would see it. Every human being is deliberately placed in the world with a purpose. You have a purpose. Even I have a purpose. We're on a mission from God.

But that doesn't mean God controls our every movement. We have free will. That means we can decide whether to accept God or reject God. But it also means we have a lot of choices. Even when we decide to go God's way, there are still so many ways to go! Look at all the saints. Some traveled the world, like St. John Paul II. Some stayed in one place, like St. Thérèse of Lisieux. Some spent their lives helping the poor, like St. Teresa of Calcutta. Some spent their lives in scholarship, like St. Jerome. There are so many ways to be a saint!

That's what I mean when I talk about life, liberty, and the pursuit of holiness. God gave you life and liberty, and pursuing holiness is what He wants you to do with those gifts. In a way, it's like you've been put in the place of Eve or Adam. But this time, you can get it right.

So let's go back to the beginning.

## The Capstone of Creation

The Bible begins with the story of creation. Actually, it begins with two stories. They differ a little in the details, but they both make the same point.

Everyone remembers the first chapter of Genesis, because it's one of the most beautiful things in the Bible. It's almost hypnotic the way this hymn of creation builds from chaos to order, with the refrain "Evening came, and morning followed—the first day.". . . "Evening came, and morning followed—the second day.". . . As you'd expect, there's an order to creation. God doesn't just fling the universe together at random. First He creates a place for everything, and then He puts everything in its place. I wish I could be that organized, but I suppose that's why nobody has offered me God's job. On the first day, God makes light. That's all, but it's necessary for everything that follows. Then, on the second day, God separates Heaven from earth by making the sky. Now we're getting somewhere. On the third day, God separates land from sea and puts plants all over the land. Now there's a place for everything—sky, sea, and land. All God has to do now is put everything in them.

So on the fourth day, God makes the Heavenly bodies—moon, sun, and stars. Now there's something to do with all that light! On the fifth day, God makes sea creatures and birds, filling the sea and the sky with life. On the sixth day, God makes all the creatures that live on land. Last of all, He makes human beings in His own image: "male and female He created them." And that's where the first story of creation ends—man and woman, the image of God, the capstone of creation. And because we are here, the world is *very good*. And God can take a rest, the Sabbath rest that seals creation and makes a covenant with the universe.

Now for another story—not a contradictory story, but a complementary one. This one starts with the creation of the man, but not the woman yet. We hear that there are no plants in the ground yet, because "there was no man to till the ground." God creates the man, and then plants a garden—Eden—and places the man in it "to cultivate and care for it."

Now remember, this is *before* sin enters the world, but humanity already has work to do. It's true that God made the world for us, but he also made us for the world. We're here to take care of God's creation.

You may have noticed that there's no woman in this story yet. The first story had man and woman made together, which we tend to forget. The story everyone remembers is the one about Eve being made from Adam's rib. But even though we remember the story, we tend to forget the context. After God places Adam in the Garden of Eden, He decides that Adam shouldn't be alone. So He makes the animals and the birds one by one, and He brings each one by to see what Adam will call it. But not one of the animals is the companion Adam needs.

Finally, God puts Adam to sleep and performs a ribectomy. "This one at last is bone of my bones and flesh of my flesh," says Adam. That's the context we often miss. The point of the story is that woman and man are the same kind of creation. All the animals are *different,* but the woman is *the same.*

## The Image and Likeness of God

Now, these two stories may seem to be different at first glance. But they reinforce each other. They have the same point—they teach us the same thing. Woman and man are the peak of creation. The world exists for us. That's why the first story builds up to the creation of human beings as the peak of God's creation. That's why the second one starts with God making human beings and then shows Him forming the world around us. They both use "figurative language," as the Catechism of the Catholic Church says, but they're telling us the same thing. God made the world for us to live in. That's really amazing, isn't it?

And, really, it's confirmed by everything we see around us. The whole universe works according to mathematical laws that hold everything together. You can walk around without floating off into space because gravity keeps pulling you toward the center of the earth. (Thanks, gravity!) But that same force of gravity keeps the earth going around the sun at just the right distance—not too close, not too far. And it keeps the sun in its place in the galaxy. And so on. If the numbers were off by just a tiny bit, the math wouldn't work, matter and energy would fall apart, and you and I would be scanning Craigslist for a new universe to live in. (Look for one with an inverse square law. Those are the best.) So it turns out that the universe really is made with you and me in mind—we couldn't exist if the rules were even a tiny bit different. And Scripture tells us that God made us in His own image. Everything else was good, but nothing else, no matter how good it might be, was made in God's image and likeness. Only the human person was made that way. That tells us something about where the meaning of life is found.

## Less than You

We live in a capitalist society, and that capitalism brings us a lot of nice things. We have houses that would make the Old Testament patriarchs shake their heads at all the wasteful luxury. We have cars that get us anywhere we want to go, most of the time. We have smartphones that are smarter than us. And yes, all those things are possible because we have money.

In fact, it's a sobering thought to realize that those Old Testament patriarchs had never heard of money. Money literally hadn't yet been invented in Abraham's time. If he wanted to buy something, he had to bring the right number of cows and goats, and maybe some doves for small change.

So, money has done some very good things for us. Nevertheless, money isn't our God. You were not made in the image and likeness of a wallet. Therefore, if you make your life all about seeking money, you will never be happy. How can I be so confident about that? Because I know that money, as good as it is, is *less than you.*

That doesn't mean money is necessarily bad. I know you hear people saying "Money is the root of all evil," but they're misquoting Scripture. The Bible doesn't say that money is the root of all evil. Rather it says, "The love of money is the root of all evils" (1 Timothy 6:10). It's great not to have to carry all those goats with me every time I go to the grocery store. Money is a good thing. It's only when we make it a God that we lose its purpose. Money is here to serve us, not for us to serve it. We're always in danger of losing sight of that because we think we don't have enough money.

All I really mean to say is this: in our society, it's *way too easy* to get obsessed with money. But money is less than you. You are made in the image of *God.* That makes the image of George Washington seem trivial, don't you think?

In fact, everything in the material world is worth less than you—except other people, because they're also made in the image of God. So your house? That's worth less than you. The car you just bought for way more money than you actually have, but that's alright because easy monthly payments take care of everything? That's worth less than you. Your phone that knows everything about you? That's worth less than you. Your baseball card collection? That's worth less than you. Even the Honus Wagner baseball card that's worth more than your house and your car and your phone put together is worth less than you. All the *things* in your life are worth less than you. And if you try to fill your unquenchable desire for meaning, reason, and purpose in everything that is worth less than you, you will *never* find what you're looking for. And you *are* looking for something. I know you are, because every human being is looking for something. What are we looking for? That question takes us back to Genesis again.

## The Talking Snake

God created human beings in his own image, Genesis tells us. And He did that out of love. Love wants to create more love. God wants to love us, and He wants us to love Him and each other. We're meant to be a constantly growing community of love.

So God placed the man and the woman in a beautiful garden where they had everything they could possibly want. The trees gave them all kinds of fruit. The animals were friendly. They had good, fulfilling work to do, tending the garden—the kind of work that makes you glad to be alive. And God Himself was their friend, who came into the garden for a nice stroll with them in the evening.

Well, we know how that worked out.

God gave us free will. We could *decide* to love Him, but we could also decide *not* to love Him. Or—because love is complicated—we could love God and still do the things He knows will make us unhappy, just because, for the moment, those things seem like more fun to us. And you know which one Adam and Eve picked.

To be fair, they had some help. "Now the snake was the most cunning of all the wild animals that the Lord God had made," we hear at the beginning of Genesis 3, and already we know where this is going. But I want you to try to imagine this scene: Adam and Eve are in the Garden of Eden, and they know there's just one rule. They can't eat the fruit of the tree of the knowledge of good and evil. Right now they don't even know what evil is! That's what the story implies. But they still have the ability to make a wrong decision—otherwise the story doesn't work. And now here comes the snake.

In every picture I've ever seen of this scene, Adam and Eve are standing by the tree—the one whose fruit they can't eat—and the snake is wound around the tree, like a big python or boa. In other words, it looks like a snake (except that in some old paintings it has a human head, which looks kind of weird).

Okay, so Adam and Eve are strolling through the garden, and this snake approaches Eve saying, "Hi! Did God *really* tell you that you couldn't eat *any* of this delicious fruit on all these lovely trees?" And Eve says, "Holy Toledo it's a talking snake!". Well, actually, she has enough presence of mind to answer the real question. But you have to imagine that the "Holy Toledo" part wasn't far back in her mind. It's scary when a snake slithers up to you and starts talking. After all, what do you call a talking snake?

Terrifying—that's what I call it.

So Eve gives the correct answer, which is, "No, we can eat anything we like. It's only this tree right here that we can't eat from. He said we'll die if we do."

Now the snake puts on his patronizing smile. (And I think if there's one thing scarier than a talking snake, it's a talking snake with a patronizing smile.) He says, "You won't die if you eat the fruit."

Of course we know the snake goes on and puts more ideas into Eve's head. "That God character is such a liar! God's just afraid that you'll be too much like Him. *He* knows all about good and evil. *You* could know, too. You could be just as smart as God if you ate that fruit."

The story in Genesis is very compact, but it does tell us a little about what was going through Eve's head at the time. She saw that the fruit looked good. It looked delicious, in fact. And gaining wisdom—how could that be a bad thing?

Well, Eve ate some of the fruit. And then she handed some to her husband, who apparently was standing *right there* the whole time, not saying anything. What was he *thinking?* (Probably something like "Holy Toledo it's a talking Snake!") And he ate the fruit, too.

## Losing Eden

The process worked as advertised. Suddenly they knew things. The first thing Adam and Eve figured out was that they were naked. It hadn't occurred to them before. Why not? Well, because there was nothing wrong with being naked. They didn't have sin, so their nakedness couldn't cause them any trouble. But now they knew what evil was. They knew that they could have evil desires as well as good ones. And the very first thing they wanted to do was cover themselves up. And then God decided to visit. So they hid.

They had never hidden before. God was their friend. Why would they hide from their friend? But anyone who's ever been a child knows the answer to that question. You love your parents, but you know when you've been bad. You know when there are going to be *consequences*. And you might just try to hide under your bed or in your closet until it all blows over. It never works, but you try it anyway, because you can't bear to face your parents, knowing what you've done. That was what happened to Adam and Eve. For the first time, they knew what guilt felt like. Congratulations! You've just learned the difference between good and evil. Don't you feel special now?

You can imagine the snake with a smug smirk on his face. Mission accomplished. Meanwhile, God is walking through the garden, saying, "Where are you? It's not like you to hide from me." And of course he finds them, because God *made* this garden. It's not like you could find a hiding place He doesn't know about.

God gives them a chance to explain themselves, and of course they botch it royally. "Well, I heard you coming, and I was naked, so . . ."

"Who told you that you were naked?" God asks. "You haven't been eating any fruit you *shouldn't* be eating, have you?"

Now here, of course, Adam could admit what he's been doing and at least make himself look a little less foolish. Instead, what does he do? Well, the same thing I probably would have done, I have to admit. He tries to deflect the blame. He blames Eve. Not only that, but he blames God. "The woman whom *you* put here with me—she gave me fruit from the tree, so I ate it."

Here's a pro tip: blaming God for your own behavior isn't going to get you very far with *anybody*, let alone God Himself.

Eve blames the snake, of course. We don't hear anything about what the snake said. Presumably, the snake was just standing there with that smug smile still on his face, because we know who that snake really was. It was Satan. Revelation will bring it all together for us: "the huge dragon, the ancient serpent, who is called the Devil and Satan, who deceived the whole world" (Revelation 12:9). Well, actions have consequences, and God has to tell the three of them what the consequences will be. Adam and Eve will endure hard work, pain, and as they'd already been warned, death. And all these consequences will be passed down to their descendants. Then Adam and Eve are tossed out of Eden, and the entrance is guarded by a flaming sword. Good luck getting past that.

Now, as the Catechism says, this story uses "figurative language." You don't have to believe that there was a literal tree with literal fruit that made one aware of good and evil. (Although you can certainly believe that, if you want to. It's a big Church.) What we do emphatically know, though, is that sin stands at the beginning of all human history, and it passes down to all of us. G.K. Chesterton once said that original sin was "the only part of Christian theology which can really be proved." All you have to do is look at human history. Can you think of anyone who wasn't a sinner? I come up with two names, and then I'm done.

Think about it. You remember that story of Adam and Eve so well precisely because it's *your* story, isn't it? It's my story, too. It's every single person's story. Think of what Paul said: "What I do, I do not understand. For I do not do what I want, but I do what I hate" (Romans 7:15). I'm like that. You're like that. Every single person in the world is like that. We know what's wrong, but we do it anyway. Why can't we do the things we know we ought to do? Why can't we be the people we know we ought to be?

## Getting Eden Back

Well, we can see the problem here. The problem is that free-will stuff. If God hadn't given us free will, we'd still be in Eden. Why couldn't God have made us so that we'd automatically do the right things? Why did He have to make it so easy for us to mess up?

The answer is that He couldn't *make* us do the right things, because then we couldn't love Him, or each other. Free will is one of the requirements for love. Liberty—that's one of God's greatest gifts to us. He gives it to us so we can really love Him, and really love each other.

From the beginning, God meant for us to be in a loving relationship with Him. We get in the most trouble when we turn away from Him and follow something else instead. Yes, He gives us that choice. God's love for you can be rejected—otherwise it wouldn't be love. It would be force.

Love needs liberty to be real love. You can't really love something that can't love you back. I may say "I love my phone," but that's not really love—I don't mean the same thing I mean when I say "I love my wife." No matter how much my phone does exactly what I tell it to do, I don't love it the same way I love Teresa. (I know Teresa has her doubts about this sometimes, but it's true.) I tell my phone what to do, and it does it (at least on a good day). And the more my phone does exactly what I tell it to do, the more it's just a *thing*. But when Teresa was my girlfriend, I didn't get down on my knee in front of her and say "You're going to marry me whether you like it or not." Trust me, that would not have worked out in my favor. I *proposed* to Teresa. It was a proposal of a *shared* life of love. And a proposal means that she had the possibility of refusing. I was very much aware that she could refuse. I was never more nervous in my life, because I knew *she could refuse*. When she said yes, I was the happiest man in the world. But it only meant something because she *could* have said no. She had free will.

This is precisely what God is doing right now to you. He's proposing a new life, one that He wants you to live with him in holiness. God wants you to be really free. The Fall in Eden made us slaves to sin. But what if we could undo that? What if we could gain back the freedom sin took from us, and this time we could make the *right* decisions? That's Christian liberty. That's the freedom we really long for. We don't always realize it, but when we say we want to be free, what we really want is to be out from under the thumb of Satan. Because its sin that keeps us from being what we know we could be. It's sin that holds us back. It binds us with iron shackles. But there's a way to cut those shackles and step out of Satan's prison into the beautiful sunlight. God has given us life. Now He's giving us liberty—real liberty. And we can use that liberty to make ourselves the people we know we can be. We don't have to just bumble through life. We can go after what we really want, and we can get it. We can be saints.

God has a plan for our lives. But, strangely enough, it's not a plan that involves just doing what God wants. That wouldn't be liberty at all. No, it's a plan for us to be exactly the people we want to be—a plan for each one of us to reach holiness in our own unique way.

God made all of us different for a reason. We can all love God and each other in different ways. And we're all headed for the same destination—Heaven—but the route there is going to be different for each one of us. But if that's true, how can God have a plan? How do we even know that He has one? Because it's been sitting right in front of us all our lives.

**FOR REFLECTION**

You are God's gift to the world. God put you here because the world wouldn't be quite right without you.

*How do I, daily, cultivate gratitude to God for the gift of my life?*

CHAPTER 2

## *God's Plan for Your Life*

WHEN I TOLD YOU THAT GOD HAD A PLAN FOR your life, how did your brain react? Did your inner voice say, "Yeah, I'd *like* to believe that, but . . ."? Did you think to yourself, "Easy for him to say, but he hasn't seen what a mess my life is"? Or did you wonder how I could possibly know about God's plan for you? Here I am saying that God has this incredible plan for your life. I'm telling you God made you for a reason. How do I know? How can I be sure God wasn't just goofing off that day?

It's a fair question. Most people reading this book have probably never met me. Some of you have (hi!), but far more of you only know me as words on a page or a face in a video. So how can I know so much about you that I know what God's plan is for you, personally?

The answer is really simple. It's smack-yourself-on-the-forehead simple. God told me. No, I don't mean I'm hearing voices, or that He sent me an angel to announce His plan for your life. (That would be kind of inefficient, wouldn't it? Better to send *you* the angel.) But God did tell me His plan. And He told you, too. God's plan for you is in the Bible. That's what the Bible is. It's the game plan for our lives. I don't just mean the New Testament, or the parts we remember from school. The entire Bible is God communicating His plan to you and me.

In fact, I really think you should be reading some of the Bible every day, if you're not doing it already. You can get one of those Bibles marked for daily reading, or you can look online for a daily reading program. The main thing is to get yourself reading the hard parts, too. If you've mostly read the same stories over and over, you've missed some amazing reading—and more importantly, you've missed some of God's plan for your life. There's a piece of that plan on every page. A good study Bible can help you see how it all fits together—how God was preparing the way for our salvation from the moment he created us, and how the story continues to the end of time. Read the Bible, all of it, over and over. The more you read, the more you'll love reading it, and the more God's plan for you, personally, will become clear to you.

The Bible covers thousands of years of stories, poetry, history, philosophy, and every kind of writing. But don't lose sight of the big picture. At the beginning, human beings are created and fall into sin. At the end, Satan is finally defeated, and the saints live joyfully forever with God. That's the story of the whole universe, but it's also the story of your own life, if you let God make it your story. God's plan is for you to be one of those joyful saints. In other words, God's plan is to make you holy.

## Holy—Not Boring

It says something about our world that when I say "holy" there's probably a part of you that thinks "boring." For some reason we think that all the *interesting* people are evil. This has been a thing in our culture for a long time. Mark Twain said, "Heaven for the climate, Hell for the company," and he was just repeating a joke that was already old in his time. You see it in movies and TV shows, too. The hero is the bland nonentity. The villain is some famous Shakespearean actor. It's as if you can't be good and interesting at the same time.

That's all backwards. Holiness is the most incredible adventure of them all. All you have to do is meet some of the real saints, and you'll realize that they're way more exciting than some has-been ham in black tights. In fact, if you keep turning these pages, you're going to meet some of the most interesting people the word has ever known, and I think you'll be amazed by how *different* they are. There's no one way to be a saint. Every saint's life is a unique adventure, and holiness is exciting because it's the only adventure that goes on for eternity.

Now, some people reading this right now probably have pretty amazing lives. Maybe you brought this book along with you while you were skydiving, because you needed something to read in the boring bit between the time you leave the plane and the time you pull the rip cord. Hello up there! I'll bet you're having fun, but you'll be on the ground in a few minutes.

Or maybe you're a tech whiz *and* financial genius, and you're about to wrangle a merger between Microsoft and Apple that will make you richer than Bill Gates *and* cooler than Steve Jobs. Sounds great! But I have two things to say to you: first, could you make Bluetooth work on my laptop? It keeps cutting out. And second, your job as CEO of Micrapplesoft is going to end. Someday it will be gone. Oh, maybe not today, and maybe not tomorrow, but soon, and for the rest of your life.

I can say these things with confidence because some day we all will be dead. Maybe not as soon as the skydiver reading my book—hey up there, did you remember to pull that cord thing?—but soon enough. And then you won't be rich anymore. You won't even be cool. You'll just be *dead*, and you'll have to deal with what you've made out of your soul. Because when you're dead, the rest of your life begins.

Then what will you do with all that money? It's not

going to do you any good. As I said, you're going to have to live with what you've made of your soul, and there are only two possible permanent destinations—Heaven or Hell. (You might have a layover in Purgatory, but you're not going to stay there forever.) *One* of those two is where you're going to be for all eternity. And you won't have any use for cash either way. Have you ever seen an ATM at a cemetery? (They do have those payday-loan places in Hell, but for some reason they always reject you.)

Well, I don't know about you, but I've seen the brochures for Hell, and I wouldn't even buy a timeshare there. I want to go to Heaven. Therefore, it's time to get holy, or die trying. And it's going to be worth it. Now is such a short time compared to all eternity! And by the way—if you die trying, I think you've made it. That's what Purgatory is for.

So, are you ready to be a saint?

## Hold On! A Saint?

Yes, a saint.

You might be thinking, "Well, yeah, I want to go to Heaven. But I don't need to *overdo* it, do I? I mean, me, a saint?" Well, that's because we get a little confused in our terminology. A saint is really anybody who's in Heaven.

I pull this trick all the time when I'm in front of an audience. I say, "How many of you expect to be saints when you die?" Only a few hands go up. Then I remind people that, in the definition of the Church, a saint is anybody who's in Heaven. Now I ask the question again: "So—how many of you expect to be saints when you die?" This time almost all the hands go up. It's a good way to reinforce the point. A saint is anybody in Heaven. We're all called to be saints, every single one of us. It's why God created us. There isn't a single one of us He made just to throw away. Every one of us has a home waiting in Heaven. "In my Father's house there are many dwelling places," Jesus told His disciples (John 14:2). "If there were not, would I have told you that I am going to prepare a place for you?"

What confuses us is that there are also *canonized* saints—saints who are on the official calendar of the Church. Those are the people we *know* are in Heaven, even with the imperfect knowledge we have here in our mortal world. But we don't know about the others yet. Most of the saints we won't ever know about until we actually get to Heaven ourselves.

What makes a person a *canonized* saint? That's a long process. To get the official recognition of the Catholic Church, you have to prove that you're in Heaven. And that means that we poor mortals down here have to want to prove that you're in Heaven, which means the process has a built-in bias toward famous Christians.

But it's a good process, with all its limitations. It

doesn't come close to telling us who *all* the saints are. But if someone has passed muster and got into the *canon*—the official list of saints—you can be completely sure that person is a saint. Most Catholics don't know much about that process. It involves a lot of people and a lot of work, but I'll give you a very rough outline. And when you've heard how it works, you'll probably see why it makes sense.

Think about it: how would you know someone was in Heaven? I mean, really know? This is important, because Catholics are going to be celebrating this person as an example of Christian virtue. We're also going to be asking for that person's intercession, meaning that we'll ask that person to pray for our intentions, on the theory that the prayers of someone who's already in Heaven must be very powerful.

So how do we know? The Church has a very specific procedure for looking into the question. And it's probably something like what you would come up with if you were trying to come up with a reliable procedure.

## How Saints Get in the Canon

First, we investigate that person's life very carefully, to see whether any unpleasant secrets are lurking. The process starts with the bishop opening a "cause" for canonization in the candidate's local diocese, and usually it doesn't start until five years after the person has died. That way the emotions surrounding the death have had a chance to simmer down, and we can look at the case more objectively. Nevertheless, the pope can remove that requirement if he thinks it's appropriate to move faster. For example, Pope John Paul II allowed the cause for Mother Teresa to start sooner. And then when John Paul himself died, his successor heard the crowds chanting "Santo subito!" ("Saint right away!") at his funeral, and decided that the people had a point.

If the local diocese, after a thorough investigation, decides that the process should be continued, it hands over all its research to the Congregation for the Causes of Saints at the Vatican. At this point, the candidate is given the title "Servant of God."

Now the Vatican experts take over, and they do an even more thorough investigation. That means going over all the evidence the local diocese got together and talking to anyone who actually knew the candidate, in case the local diocese has missed anybody. There's even a special official called the Promoter of the Faith whose job is to argue against the canonization of the would-be saint. We used to call him the Devil's Advocate, because he's kind of like a lawyer for the opposition. But that doesn't mean he's really on the side of the devil: it just means the people at the Vatican are really serious about doing their job thoroughly.

Now, let's suppose we've talked to everyone, from the first-grade teacher to the nurse on duty when our candidate died, and no one can tell us anything that would keep us from thinking this person was a saint. We've read everything the candidate wrote, maybe looked at all the YouTube videos the candidate left behind, and there's nothing in there that anyone could object to. The Congregation for the Causes of Saints sends their verdict to the pope, and usually the pope accepts their verdict. Now the candidate has passed the second stage, and the Church calls that person "Venerable."

Well, that's great—but it's not proof. After all, God judges us on the contents of our hearts, and even if our candidate did everything right on the outside, mortals like us can't see into other people's hearts. What we need is proof that the person actually is in Heaven. And unless the candidate was a martyr (someone who died for the faith, which is like the express lane to Heaven), we don't have that slam-dunk proof. But what if we could design a sort of scientific experiment to tell us what we want to know?

No, we're not going to go up to Heaven and set up a lab. The last time we tried to build our way up to Heaven, the project bogged down in communications problems, and they finally cut off the funding (see Genesis 11). But we do have a way of communicating with Heaven. It's called the Communion of Saints. All the souls in Purgatory and Heaven, and all the faithful on earth, are bound together in mutual love. That means that the saints in Heaven don't stop caring about us just because they're in Heaven.

So, back to our candidate for sainthood: we can ask for that person's prayers in a seemingly impossible situation. If God decides to grant that prayer through the candidate's intercession, then we have some real evidence.

It's important to remember that this is up to God. If God doesn't answer our prayers the way we were hoping for, that doesn't mean the person isn't in Heaven. It may just mean that we don't know what God's plan is. So our experiment can come up with a lot of false negatives. But we're not going to get false positives, because every claim of a miracle is rigorously investigated. The Vatican has experts on call for this sort of thing. If it's a medical miracle, the medical specialists look into it, and they search for any possible natural explanation of the cure. (Most claimed miracles don't even make it through this investigation.) But let's suppose God comes through with a miracle in response to our candidate's intercession. Great! That's the third stage. Now we can call that person "Blessed." Only one more approved miracle is needed to make our candidate a canonized saint.

And it happens. The final miracle has been approved. Now, everything is in place. The miracles have been investigated, the pope declares our candidate a saint, and the name is officially entered into the canon of saints, with a feast day and everything. Now we can name parishes after that person, and Catholics all over the world are encouraged to turn to that person for help.

That's how you get into the canon. As you can see, there's a lot to the process. So it's important to remember that, just because the process is so involved, the saints in the canon are only a tiny fraction of the saints actually in Heaven.

## But What about Me?

So you may not be headed for the canon of saints. (Although you may be. Don't count yourself out yet.) But God does have a plan to make you a saint in the only way that matters; by bringing you to be with Him in Heaven forever.

"But who am I to go to Heaven?" you may be thinking.

You're you! That's the answer. God made you because He wanted *you* to be with Him. You'll be happy to know that saints come in all shapes and sizes. In fact, I could tell you about canonized saints who lived extraordinary lives. These are some of the most heroic tales of adventure you will ever hear—tales that make all those swashbuckling adventure movies look tame.

But I could also tell you about canonized saints who

led incredibly normal lives like yours and mine. They just did the normal with an extra shot of love. (That's why I told you not to count yourself out of the canon yet. Even if you've never done anything exciting at all, you'll fit right in.)

Some saints were wildly successful in their earthly voyages; some saints failed miserably. Some saints were kings and queens; others were doorkeepers and dishwashers. Some were out amongst the people; others were hidden away in a cloister. Some traveled around the world, and some never left their beds.

But they all had one thing in common: they knew that holiness was the most important thing, not worldly success, and definitely not money. It was faith. Nothing got in the way of that, and nothing should get in our way, either.

That's why it's so important to remember that a saint is anyone in Heaven. If God wants you canonized, that's up to Him. But it shouldn't matter to you. What should matter to you is Heaven.

Do you have a mission statement for your life? If it's not "to become a saint," it's the wrong mission statement. "To become a saint" should be the mission statement of every single human being. It's my mission statement, my wife's mission statement, and my kids mission statement. Seriously. If you ask my kids right now what their mission statement is, they will tell you, "to become a saint." Is that because they are exceptionally holy? Nope. They're normal kids. But they know their mission statement because I remind them about it almost every day. I don't ever want them to forget it, because nothing can be more important than that.

Alright, let's say I've convinced you (and I don't see why not). It's either Heaven or Hell (when I put it that way, most people agree it's an easy choice). So I'm going to assume that you want to be a saint, meaning someone who ends up in Heaven for all eternity. Now, you might ask me, how do I know I'm headed in the right direction? This is where the canonized saints are very helpful. We know they're in Heaven, right? So one good way of knowing if you're heading in the right direction—the direction of holiness—is by looking at the canonized saints. This is why I share stories about their lives in all of my books. Don't think this book is going to be any different: I'm going to share some examples in this one, too. Because what we need in our world today more than anything else are *examples* of holiness. I will never tire of saying it: the saints' lives *change* lives.

I'm so glad we have so many saints to turn to! In fact, one canonized saint is responsible for a lot of the saints in the canon. St. John Paul II canonized more saints than *five centuries* of his predecessors combined. Think about that! Five hundred years of popes didn't canonize as many saints as St. John Paul II did in his quarter of a century as pope. He gave the Church so many treasures to look to for guidance. And he didn't do it by relaxing the standards. He did it by making it a priority to look for good examples.

## New Saints for New Times

Some of them were famous people. Some of them you've probably never heard of, like **St. Angela of the Cross**, for example. She didn't live all that long ago; in fact, she died in 1932, and she spent a good part of her life working in a shop that repaired shoes.

Now, you wouldn't think there would be many opportunities to be exceptionally holy at a shoe-repair shop (there's a pun there somewhere), but Angela had one luxury that not everyone who works in the retail sector can have: she had a great boss. Her boss was very religious, and she encouraged the people who worked for her to read the lives of the saints and pray together.

Twice, Angela tried to become a nun. Once the order rejected her because she wasn't healthy enough, the other time she got in but got so sick that she had to go home. So it was back to the shoe shop.

But she never gave up on what she really wanted to do, which was devote her life to helping the poor. Finally, when she was 29 years old, Angela got two other women together and founded her own order. This time her health held out, and she was able to spend the rest of a good long life (she lived to be 86) taking care of the poor and sick, expanding her order along the way to about two dozen convents in Spain.

St. Angela found her way to holiness working in a shoe shop. That would have pleased another, more famous saint canonized by Pope John Paul: **St. Josemaria Escriva**, who founded Opus Dei—"the Work of God." Finding holiness in everyday work is what Opus Dei is all about.

Josemaria (his father was named Jose, and his mother was named Maria) was very sick as a child, and he believed he only lived because of his parents' prayers to Our Lady. He was especially devoted to Mary for the rest of his life.

He became a priest, but when he was in his middle 20s, he suddenly saw that he had a special vocation. He saw that what the world needed was not necessarily more priests or religious, but more *ordinary people* acting as if they were meant to be saints. Why shouldn't you be a holy engineer, or a holy plumber, or a holy shoe-repair worker, or a holy carpenter (like somebody you might remember)?

Today the organization St. Josemaria founded has members all over the world, and his ideas were a big part of Vatican II's emphasis on the call to holiness for all believers. In many ways, you could say the Catholic Church today is what it is because of St. Josemaria's vision.

Well, I've mentioned two saints from Spain, but I don't want you to think that all the saints John Paul canonized came from Europe. How about one from Sudan? **St. Josephine Bakhita** came from Darfur, where as a child she was captured by slaver owners and sold, and sold again, and sold again, until she finally ended up being sold to the Italian consul in Sudan. When the consul went back to Italy, he took Josephine with him, and then gave her away to one of his friends.

In her new family, Josephine was governess for a little girl who was being instructed in the Catholic faith. Learning about the faith from the sisters who were instructing her charge, Josephine herself converted.

When her owners wanted to take her back to Sudan, Josephine wouldn't go. Her mistress tried to force her, and even tried to get the legal system on her side, which didn't work out very well. The sisters who had taught Josephine intervened on her behalf. So did the cardinal archbishop of Venice. The court ruled that Italian law didn't recognize slavery, so Josephine was not and had never been a slave. She was free to do what she wanted, and what she wanted to do was join the sisters.

Josephine spent the rest of her life—more than half a century longer—as a nun, earning the love of all the people the sisters served. By the time she died in 1947, the people in town already thought she was a saint. It just took the rest of the Church a few decades to catch up.

**St. Agnes Tsao Kou Ying** was a Chinese martyr whose crime was preaching the Christian faith to her neighbors.

In the 1800s, it was illegal for European missionaries to venture into the interior of China; in fact, Europeans could only come to a few port cities. But missionaries had been coming to China for hundreds of years anyway, because you can't keep Christians from spreading the Gospel.

Agnes was born to Catholic parents. She married a farmer, but her husband's relatives hated her for being a Christian. When her husband died, they threw her out of the house and left her homeless.

Fortunately, Agnes met another good Catholic woman who took her in, and together the two of them studied Catholic doctrine and the Scriptures. When one of the traveling missionaries came by, he found that Agnes knew her Catholic doctrine very well, and he asked her to come with him and help teach some of the converts in Guangxi.

That was what she was doing when the Christians in the area were rounded up. Most of them were released, but Agnes was one of the ringleaders in the eyes of the local judge. He did everything he could to persuade her to renounce her faith, but finally had her tortured to death by sticking her in a tiny cage where she couldn't move. It took her three days to die, praying the whole time. Like the ancient Roman martyrs, she could have avoided that just by renouncing Christ. But she chose holiness. She decided she wanted to be a saint.

How about a saint from North America? **St. Juan Diego** is famous as the man Mary appeared to in Mexico. Our Lady of Guadalupe is the symbol of the Mexican church and the patroness of Latin America. Literally millions of people converted because of Juan Diego's vision and the miraculous image of Mary on his cloak.

You've probably heard his story. Juan Diego was born in Mexico before the Europeans arrived. After Cortez and the Spanish conquered Mexico, the missionaries weren't making much progress—mostly because the Spanish conquerors were brutally oppressive. (The landowners often threatened the missionaries when they tried to stand up for the conquered population.) Juan Diego was one of the few converts. He used to go frequently to take catechism lessons. One day, while he was walking toward the bishop's house, Our Lady appeared to him with a message for the bishop. She wanted him to build a chapel where her people could pray.

Of course the bishop didn't believe Juan Diego's story. Eventually Our Lady gave him a sign: roses blooming in the middle of winter. She told him to gather a bunch and take them to the bishop. Juan Diego carried them in his cloak— and when he dumped them out in front of the bishop, there was Our Lady's image where the roses had been.

Juan Diego was just a good Christian pursuing holiness in his own way. He wasn't looking for an apparition from Our Lady—but he was ready and willing to respond when she called him. It seems strange that the image of Our Lady of Guadalupe has been venerated for hundreds of years, but the man she appeared to wasn't canonized until my lifetime! Sometimes the Church moves awfully slowly. But what's a few hundred years against eternity?

Finally, I'll mention one saint from right here in my own United States. **St. Rose Philippine Duchesne** is one of my favorites to bring up, because most people would have said she was a failure. She came from France to the American frontier in 1818, settling in Missouri, which had only recently been bought from France as part of the Louisiana Purchase. Rose's dream was to spend her life teaching the Native Americans about the Gospel.

Her problem was that she could never really learn their language. Native American languages are totally different from Indo-European languages like English or French. Some of the early missionaries had an amazing gift for learning languages, and managed to speak the American languages like natives. Rose wasn't one of them.

So she could never really teach, because she couldn't make herself understood. All she could do was pray. She prayed all the time. In fact, the other missionaries felt as though she held up their whole operation with her prayers, and the Native American converts were amazed and impressed by how much time she spent praying. But Rose always felt as though she'd failed.

Eventually her health gave out, and she had to go back to the relative civilization of St. Charles, the big town in the territory, where she stayed in a tiny room all alone and prayed. She died years later, never having been able to live her life's ambition of being a great teacher to the Native Americans. Failure? Well, now she's a canonized saint. There you go—half a dozen saints out of almost 500 canonized by St. John Paul II while he was pope. They couldn't be more different. Some were fabulously successful. Some were very humble. There's no one way to be holy. In fact there are as many ways to be holy as there are people on earth, because God made each one of us to be a saint, in our own way.

Mother Teresa—now St. Teresa of Calcutta—was once asked, "Mother, how can I become a saint?" Her hilarious response was, "Go to Rome. Pope John Paul II is canonizing everyone!"

But I have a better answer. (I know: I have a better answer than a canonized saint! I'm going to have to work on that pride stuff. But anyway . . . ). It's fun to go to Rome, but you don't have to go there because Rome will come to you.

**FOR REFLECTION**

One good way of knowing if you're heading in the right direction – the direction of holiness – is by looking at the canonized saints.

*Which (canonized) saint am I most interested in learning more about? Why?*

## CHAPTER 3

# So, Why the Catholic Church?

S O YOU WANT TO BE A SAINT. I think I can take that for granted now that we've established that a saint is anyone in Heaven. The alternative is Hell, which is nobody's favorite neighborhood. So what now?

Remember Mother Teresa's answer. Somebody asked her, "Mother, how can I become a saint?" She answered, "Go to Rome. Pope John Paul II is canonizing everyone!" It was a joke of course, but I think there's a serious point buried in it.

The Roman Catholic Church—the Church with its heart in Rome—is one giant saint-making machine. The Church exists for only one reason, and that's to make a saint of every single person in the world. That's why I'm Catholic. No, not because it's easy (it's certainly not). Not because it's filled with perfect people (we know all too well that's not true). I'm Catholic because I believe it's in and through the Catholic Church that I have the best chance of becoming a saint—meaning that being Catholic gives me the best chance of being in Heaven with God for all eternity. And I can assure you that if I didn't believe that, I wouldn't be Catholic. The Church offers the winning game plan. And we do need a game plan, don't we? We're not in this fight on our own.

Think of what it would be like if a football coach told his offense to go out on this drive and just run whatever play they thought would work. You'd have the right guard blocking in pass-protection, while the left guard was blocking as if it was a run play. One wide receiver would go deep looking for the ball, the quarterback would be thinking screen, and the running back would be driving the Zamboni. It would be total chaos. You need a plan to win this game. That's precisely what the Church offers us.

But wait! Why should I think the Catholic Church has the only game plan? There are lots of playbooks out there, aren't there? There are Protestants of all kinds. There are Muslims and Hindus and Buddhists. There are new-agers who think the secret is that we should all just be, like, *mindful*, man.

And it may surprise you to hear me say this, but I expect to meet a lot of those people in Heaven. Many in our secular society never really hear the message of the Gospel. It's not their fault; all they get is the distorted version of Christianity they see in popular entertainment. And frankly, I wouldn't like those Christians either if that was what they were really like. Nevertheless, those people can hear God calling them, because God calls every single one of us. And some of them will answer the call, somehow. (See a very thoughtful explanation of our relationship to other religions in the Catechism of the Catholic Church, paragraphs 839–848.) But they're going to have an uphill battle, because they'll have to work out for themselves what the Church could just give them: the route to Heaven.

Doesn't it seem awfully arrogant to say that only the Catholic Church has the route to Heaven, the plan to win the game, the fullness of truth about God? Actually, I don't think it's arrogant at all. In fact, after I've explained a few things, I think you'll see that it would be arrogant *not* to let the Church point us to Heaven.

## Founding a Movement

When Jesus ascended into Heaven, He didn't leave His disciples without any guidance. He knew His people were going to need a lot of help finding their way along the path to holiness, so He had already put a lot of effort into making them ready to take over leading his movement on earth. In fact, He had already founded the Catholic Church.

First of all, He picked one of the disciples to be the leader. You've heard the story many times (it's in Matthew 16:13–20). Jesus asked the disciples what people were saying about Him. Well, they answered, "Some say you're John the Baptist, and some say you're Elijah, and some say you're Jeremiah or one of the prophets."

"But who do you say that I am?" Jesus asked.

One of them had the answer. It was Peter. "You are the Messiah, the Son of the living God."

That was the moment when Jesus revealed his plan for Peter. "And so I say to you, you are Peter" (a name that means "Rock"), "and upon this rock I will build my church, and the gates of the netherworld shall not prevail against it."

Now, Peter didn't necessarily seem like the obvious choice. If you and I wanted a leader for a new organization, we'd look for someone who had some business experience. We'd want someone who knew something about organizational leadership and had a good education. It would also help if he had some connections—you know, if he knew people in high places. Looking over all the disciples, I think the one I would have picked for the job would have been Judas Iscariot. (Yeah, I'm not always a perfect judge of character.)

But Peter? Seriously? He never missed a chance to make a fool of himself. Nevertheless, he was Jesus's choice. And I've always thought that Jesus deliberately picked the goof-up among His disciples, because it was His way of showing us He wouldn't leave us alone. I'm going to take *this guy,* He said, and I'm going to give him so much strength that no one will be able to budge this Church no matter how hard they try.

Alright, so we have a leader. But he's one among twelve. They're all going to have to work together on this, and each one of them is going to have to take on a lot of responsibility as the movement grows. So already we've got twelve overseers, one of whom will be the overseer of the overseers. By the way, the Greek word for "overseer" is *episkopos,* which is the word that gives us our English word "bishop."

Next, we need a vision statement. Every good organization needs a vision statement. And Jesus didn't leave us in the lurch there, either.

"Go, therefore, and make disciples of all nations, baptizing them in the name of the Father, and of the Son, and of the Holy Spirit, teaching them to observe all that I have commanded you." Christ's vision for his Church was to baptize every single person in the world! That's right at the end of the Gospel of Matthew.

"All nations huh, Jon? He couldn't have scaled that down a bit? Like, 'Go and make disciples of, oh, say, Palestine and a bit of Syria, and maybe northeastern Egypt, and, hey, that'll make me proud of you.'" No, it was going to be the whole world. And the twelve overseers were going to have to teach, too. But, once again, Jesus had planned ahead. Not only had He spent His whole ministry teaching, but after He rose from the dead He gave his disciples a 40-day intensive course. They knew what they had to teach.

But still, bringing that message to the whole world was going to be a tall order, especially when the world didn't want to hear it. But Jesus had promised to send His Spirit to keep His messengers going, to give them the power they needed when they tackled the impossible tasks ahead of them. That was what happened on the day of Pentecost. The Holy Spirit came to the twelve apostles with powerful demonstrations. Speaking in every language! I have trouble enough with English some days. They made 3000 converts that one day. Till that time, they'd just been sitting in the room where they'd had the Last Supper, praying for something to happen. I guess their prayers were answered.

So that's the foundation story of the Church. Jesus set up an administration, gave them the rule book, and then sent the Holy Spirit to be the actual power behind his Church. And if you're thinking I left out the most important thing He did, you're absolutely right. But we'll get to that in a moment.

## Building the Catholic Church

The book of the Acts of the Apostles tells us how that early Church prospered against all odds. First we see how the Way, as the Christians called their new movement, spread through Judea and Galilee, and then into Samaria, and then up into Syria, and then into Asia Minor and Greece. By the time the book ends, Paul is in Rome, the heart of the world, and possibly on his way to Spain, the western end of the world.

That's just the generation of the first apostles. But this Church was going to have to go on generation after generation, till the end of time. When would the end of time be? No one could tell. As far as the apostles knew, it might be thousands of years from their time, or it might be that day. The Church would have to live as if Jesus were coming right away, and it would have to be organized as if He might not come for a long, long time.

There was another motivation for the apostles to think about how the Church would do without them: powerful people wanted to kill them. They had killed Jesus, after all (though that didn't work out too well for them), and they had killed Stephen. Soon, they would try to kill the apostles.

One by one, they succeeded. One of the Jameses was first to go: King Herod had him killed and saw that some people liked it, so he went after the Christians even more.

(This wasn't Herod the Great, the mad tyrant who was king when Jesus was born, but one of his sons—we could call him Herod the Not-So-Great.)

Of course, these persecutions had the opposite effect of what the authorities intended. When they killed Stephen, for example, the Christians scattered all over the countryside—founding churches wherever they went. Instead of destroying the little Christian movement, the persecution spread it all over the place. That kept happening. It especially kept happening after one of the fiercest persecutors, Saul of Tarsus, was converted by a miraculous vision of Christ himself. Saul, also known as Paul (see Acts 13:9), became the most vigorous evangelist of the new faith. Naturally, people wanted to kill him, too. Knowing they could die at any moment, the apostles took care to make sure the Church could go on without them.

First of all, there was already a lot of work to do—far more than thirteen men (counting Paul) could do. To take care of some of the important duties like tending to the poor and the widows, the apostles appointed helpers. The Greek word for "helper" is *diakonos,* from which we get our English word "deacon."

As leaders of local congregations, the apostles appointed elders—men who were respected in the Christian community and could take on the duties of leading the congregation in worship. The Greek word for "elder" is *presbyter,* from which we get our English word "priest."

Finally, to take the place of the apostles in other cities, and to replace them when they were gone, the apostles appointed overseers to lead the whole Christian community in one area. As we've already seen, the Greek word for "overseer" is *episkopos*, from which we get our English word "bishop."

Deacon, priest, bishop: in the Acts of the Apostles, we see the structure of the Catholic Church today. That structure hasn't changed since the time when the Twelve-plus-Paul were still alive.

From then on, it was all smooth sailing, right? I mean, the structure of the Church was already in place, the Holy Spirit was there to guide her, and the persecutions only made more Christians. What could go wrong?

Well . . .

## Not Quite Smooth Sailing

I've always been fascinated by the story of the early Church. I think what fascinates me is that it's a *story*. It has heroes and villains, and it has conflicts and emotions and all the things that make for a good story. It's obvious that God had a plan for His Church. We can see its progress through history, and even though there are a lot of major bumps in the road, we can see that it's headed along the route God mapped out for it.

So, yes, there's a plan. And since it's God's plan, you might think this plan just came together easily. But anyone who's ever read a paragraph of Church history knows it was a glorious and arduous task, and the plan didn't come together easily at all.

First of all, many people wanted to get rid of the Christians—but as we see, their persecutions had the opposite effect. "You make more of us when you cut us down," said one famous early Christian. "The blood of Christians is seed." (It's from Tertullian's *Apology*. The actual Latin is "Plures efficimur, quitiens metimur a vobis: semen est sanguis Christianorum," if you know Latin, or if you're like me and can get somebody to help you with Latin.) You often hear it quoted as "the blood of the martyrs is the seed of the Church."

Then, other people accepted Christianity, but chose to twist its message into whatever they wanted it to be. We call people like that "heretics," from a Greek word that means "choosing," and was often used to mean forming factions like political parties.

We already see some of these people in the New Testament: think of St. Jude warning the Christians about false teachers. "These people are complainers, disgruntled ones who live by their desires; their mouths utter bombast as they fawn over people to gain advantage" (Jude 16).

Some of these heretics went wrong in one little difference from Christian teaching. Some of them went way off the deep end. But I think they actually served an important purpose in God's plan for the Church. By making stuff up like that, they forced the Church to be very much aware of what the real Christian teaching was. They forced the best thinkers in the Church to analyze the teaching of the Church and make it clearer, so that Christians would know exactly what Christ really meant by his teachings.

## Some of the More Notable Heresies

Each heresy was defined by the way it deviated from the right teaching, which is what we call *orthodoxy* (from a Greek word meaning "right teaching," so you see this theology stuff isn't always so hard once you get the hang of it). Here are just a few of them:

**Gnosticism** covered a wide variety of sects, but the thing they all had in common was that they all believed there was a *secret* teaching of Jesus just for the few really smart people like, oh, say, the Gnostics. In fact the word "Gnostic" comes from the Greek word for "knowing," which actually has the same ancient ancestor as our English word "knowing." (You can see the family resemblance in *gno-* and *kno-*.)

*Where the Gnostics went wrong:* The teaching of Christ is for everybody. There's not one teaching for regular people and another for the very few (that you can have for only eight easy payments of $29.99). It's always the same teaching, everywhere and at all times.

**Docetism** was the idea that Christ only *seemed* to die on the Cross. He had some sort of fake body to put on the cross, while the real Christ stood by and laughed.

*Where the Docetists went wrong:* Christ's death was a real death. It would have had no redemptive value if it hadn't been. Jesus really did give His life for us, and He suffered everything a human being could suffer, including complete biological death. Many of the Gnostics held Docetist beliefs.

The **Ebionites** believed that Christians had to follow the complete Jewish law, including all the dietary restrictions and the rituals.

*Where the Ebionites went wrong:* Jesus came to fulfill the law. Once that had been accomplished by his sacrifice, the purpose of all the rituals was gone. In their place was the one perfect sacrifice for the forgiveness of sins.

**Marcionite,** named for its founder Marcion, taught that the God of the Old Testament was a different being from the God of the New Testament. The world had been created by an evil creator God, and we were his slaves. Therefore, of course, all material creation was evil. Jesus had come to introduce us to the good God we had never heard of before and free us from the evil creator of the universe. Naturally, Marcionites didn't accept the Old Testament as Scripture.

*Where the Marcionites went wrong:* The world God created—though it's messed up by our sin—is very good, as Genesis told us. Jesus Himself taught from the Old Testament Scriptures. You can't understand Christianity without understanding how it came out of the Jewish thought of the Old Testament.

**Arianism,** named for its founder Arius, taught that the Son was an inferior being created by the Father. The Nicene Creed was a response to Arianism. When we say "God from God, Light from Light, true God from true God, begotten, not made, consubstantial with the Father," and so on, it may seem that we're belaboring the point, but all those terms are in there because they respond precisely to what the Arians believed.

*Where the Arians went wrong:* God the Son and God the Father are two persons of the same God, equal in every way. If you deny that, you lose the whole point of the Incarnation: that God Himself came to us and actually died as a human being, because that was the only thing that could save us.

**Macedonianism** (named after some guy named Macedonius, not after Macedonia) refused to accept the Holy Spirit as a person of the Trinity. Our Creed has the words "And in the Holy Spirit ... who with the Father and the Son is worshiped and glorified" because of the Macedonians.

*Where the Macedonians went wrong:* The Holy Spirit is just as much God as the Father and the Son. When God sends us the Holy Spirit to guide us, that's God himself coming into our Church and our hearts.

This is just a short list out of the dozens or maybe hundreds of heretical groups that popped up over the first few centuries of the Church. Most of them had some limited success in small areas and then faded away, but some got to be big problems. The worst problem was probably the Arians, because for many years the Roman Emperors were Arian, which put the power of the imperial government on the Arian side.

Nevertheless, I think you can begin to see why I said there was a purpose to these heretical groups. Each one of them forced the Church to think about and define an important doctrine that had been implicit in Jesus' teaching, but hadn't been properly expressed yet. They were like chisels against a piece of marble: when they seemed to be doing the most damage, they were actually making the marble into a beautiful sculpture.

## The Refiner's Fire

Heresies kept things interesting on the outside, but there were also plenty of arguments on the inside—arguments that didn't flare up into full-scale heresies or schisms. (A *schism* is a division in the Church where the two sides may not necessarily believe different things, but they're still separated. It's like two people living in the same house refusing to talk to each other.) The Church stayed together, but the fireworks could be pretty spectacular.

Often, you'd have two really holy saints on the opposite side of a very important issue. Some would argue ferociously. Others would call names with wild tempers flaring. St. Jerome was good at that—he was like the Don Rickles of the Church Fathers. If he disagreed with you, he could come up with a colorful insult to put you in your place. Believe it or not, he had a long fight with St. Augustine, carried out in letters, so we still have the whole thing. And yet St. Augustine is one of the most important theologians in the Catholic Church, and St. Jerome was the translator of the Vulgate, the Latin version of the Bible that's still the standard for the Catholic Church. These are two of the most important figures in Christian history, but their long spite-fest is permanently recorded in the pages of history. I wouldn't have it any other way. Part of the miracle of the Catholic Church is that it has survived fallible human beings like you and me over 2000 years of history, and it's by far the largest religious organization on the planet.

Now, when Jerome and Augustine were fighting (and that's just one example—saints arguing happened more often than you'd think), they could have left the conversation altogether. They could have stomped off in opposite directions. Each one could have refused to have anything to do with a church that included *that man*. But they didn't. They knew this plan of faith was important for the salvation of souls.

Obviously, there have been times when people did leave the Catholic Church. We still haven't completely reconciled with the Eastern Orthodox churches, for example, and the Protestant Reformation took away a lot of people. But we see that through history—and this is true right up to today—the great majority of Christians have stayed in the Catholic Church. That's what "Catholic" *means*, after all; it's from a Greek word meaning "universal." The Catholic Church is the one that's meant to be the church for everybody.

That means the saints who disagreed with each other didn't go off and form their own churches. A saint who thought the Church was going in the wrong direction would do all he could to rescue the Church. He might lose his temper because (and I know this sounds weird, but it's true), saints are sinners, too. But he wouldn't think of leaving the Catholic Church. I guess it's fair to ask: why not? Was it just inertia? An American like me is used to comparison shopping. If I'm in one store and I can't get what I want at the price I want, I'll go across the street. Or I'll buy it online. Similarly, if the church I'm going to doesn't seem lively enough, I'll go to the megachurch where the music and preaching is better.

But the saints have all known that the Catholic Church can't be replaced. You can't just pick another church and get the same results. And that's because the Catholic Church has what all those other churches are missing.

And now, at last, we come back to the most important thing Jesus left His apostles—the one I left out all those pages ago.

### Don't Forget the Sacraments!

One of the things I'm fond of saying today is that we would do well to get back to the basics of our faith. If you've heard me talk about it before, you know what I mean by the basics. I mean the sacraments.

Why do I care so much about the sacraments? It's because they have *power*. They're not just symbolic rituals. They actually give us the strength we need to go on when we're flagging in our pursuit of holiness. Here's how the

Catechism of the Catholic Church defines the sacraments (in paragraph 1131):

"The sacraments are efficacious signs of grace, instituted by Christ and entrusted to the Church, by which divine life is dispensed to us."

That's dense. It's so dense you probably yawned. But now let me tell you why this is maybe the most exciting sentence in the whole Catechism. It's certainly the most exciting sentence in *my* book. I'm going to pick through it phrase by phrase.

First: "efficacious signs of grace." Those four words pack a lot of meaning!

Grace is a huge idea itself. Grace is all the things God gives us, not because we deserve them, but because God loves us. It's hard for us to imagine—and yet I think you might have some little hint of an idea if you've ever been a parent. Think of when your baby was just a few weeks old. You did *everything* for that kid. Was it because she deserved it? Of course not. A baby hasn't done anything to *deserve* your love. You just love her.

So the sacraments are signs of grace. They tell us how much God loves us.

But wait! They're not just *signs* of grace. They're *efficacious* signs of grace. That means they actually *do* the things they're signs of. What do I mean by that? I mean they have *power*—power to make us holy, which is what we're after.

Think about the Sacrament of Reconciliation—the one we usually call confession. We confess our sins, and then the priest gives us the sign that we're forgiven. But it's not just a sign. With that sacrament, we actually do receive complete forgiveness of our sins. The sacrament does the thing it's a sign of. It's *efficacious*. After we've dirtied ourselves up with our sins, this sacrament literally makes us holy again.

Isn't that amazing? Think about what we have at our disposal! The ability to know, without a shadow of a doubt, that upon absolution in the Sacrament of Reconciliation we are completely forgiven. How do we know that? Because Jesus told His disciples, "Receive the holy Spirit. Whose sins you forgive are forgiven them, and whose sins you retain are retained." If you've ever wondered why the priest speaks in the first person when he's granting absolution—why he says "*I* absolve you from your sins in the name of the Father, and of the Son, and of the Holy Spirit," not "*Jesus* absolves you"—that's why. Because it's not just him speaking, it's Jesus speaking through him. That's why he wears that stole around his neck. Our priests aren't just playing dress-up. That stole represents the authority Christ Jesus gave to his disciples. When that priest was ordained, he received that authority through the bishop, who had received it from a bishop, and so on in an unbroken chain back to the original apostles who received it from Christ. How incredible is that?

## Substance and Accidents

Jesus also gives us His body and blood. We receive His body and blood in the bread and wine of the Eucharist. We see, taste, smell, and feel bread and wine. But it's His body and blood, soul and divinity, really, truly, and substantially present in the *accidents* of bread and wine.

That philosophical distinction needs a little explanation. Catholic philosophers have followed the ancient Greek thinker Aristotle in making a distinction between the *substance* of a thing and its *accidents*. This isn't science, which deals only with material things. It's a way of talking about the ideas that are out of reach of science. The *substance* is what the thing really is—its actual being. The *accidents* are the appearances, the smells, the textures, that are apparent to the senses. Those accidents can change without making a difference in the substance.

For example, imagine an apple. What does it look like in your imagination? It could be a deep red Jonathan apple, or a Golden Delicious, or a bright green Granny Smith. Green, golden, red—those are all *accidents*, in the philosophical Aristotelian sense. They describe what the thing looks like. But the thing really *is* an apple. It may be sweet, tart, sour—all those things are also accidents. It's still an apple. Its appleness is its *substance*.

I can change the accidents of the apple, too. For example, I could dye a Granny Smith so it looks like a Jonathan.

I don't know why I would, but I could if I wanted to. It would still be a Granny Smith apple, although it would be a weird Granny Smith that probably nobody would want. In the Eucharist, the substance changes, but the accidents stay the same. Catholic philosophers describe this with the word *transubstantiation*, which is basically Latin for "the substance changes, but the accidents stay the same." So the bread and wine are still bread and wine only to our senses. They're not really bread and wine anymore. Once the priest has consecrated those elements, they actually are the body and blood of Christ. There's real power there, the most important power we could ever experience. Because God won't hold back anything to help us get to where He wants us to be, which is with Him in Heaven.

What that means is this: in no other church around the world will you be able to get closer to God than in the Catholic Church. Because in no other Church around the world do they proclaim transubstantiation. Remember that word. It's a big word, but it's important to know. It explains one of the core differences between Catholics and most other kinds of Christians (not including the Orthodox, who believe the same thing expressed in different words).

If someone asks you why you're a Catholic, instead of belonging to that megachurch by the mall with three laser light shows every Sunday, you now have an answer. The show can't compare. Catholics have something way more exciting than that. We have Jesus Christ right there on the altar, ready to give us His own body and blood so we'll have the strength to follow the road to Heaven. All they have is a preacher who shouts a lot.

It's worth pointing out again that this goes all the way back to the teaching of Christ. When Jesus said "this is my body" and "this is my blood," He meant what He said. But it's in the Catholic Church that we've kept that teaching pure, without softening it for popular consumption. And we couldn't have done it without all those saints arguing. So good job, saints! I thank God so many of you did the heavy lifting for us today.

But the plan isn't nearly over. God continues to give us new plays to run to make us holy. Holiness is really all about freedom—freedom from the things that hold us back—the things that stand in our way on the road to eternal happiness. God knows we can't fight those things by ourselves. So He gives us the Church too, so we can be free—truly free. However, that freedom is different from what most of us mean when we say "freedom" today. So we're going to have to think hard about what we really mean when we say "freedom."

———

Engage, inspire, and awaken your parish with Jon Leonetti's Surge of the Heart parish mission! Learn more at www.JonLeonetti.com

**FOR REFLECTION**

I'm Catholic because I believe it's in and through the Catholic Church that I have the best chance of becoming a saint – meaning that being Catholic gives me the best chance of being in Heaven with God for all eternity.

*If someone were to ask you why you're Catholic, how would you respond?*

## CHAPTER 4

# The Battle for Liberty

GIVE ME LIBERTY, OR GIVE ME DEATH! EVERYBODY remembers that great rallying cry of the American Revolution: it came from a speech by Patrick Henry. Well, in this chapter, I want to help you understand that the American notion of freedom and Christian freedom are two very different things. They're both very good things. But one of them is better. Guess which one I'm thinking of?

All right, I know. I'm not even making it hard. You know I'm going to tell you that Christian freedom is better. But I'm going to tell you *why* I think that, and I think you'll agree with me once you understand what I'm talking about.

## Freedom and *Freedom*

The foundation of the United States was one of the most important events in the history of the world. I truly believe that when we won our independence, it changed the whole history of the world for the better. Just look around the world today. Every country either operates on our American principles or *pretends* to operate on our American principles. Practically everyone at least pretends to guarantee freedom of religion. Practically everyone at least pretends to guarantee freedom of speech.

Of course, every country finds ways around those freedoms (hey, I know we're not perfect either, but we're trying), but most everybody (unfortunately *not* everybody) agrees that they're good things to have, and you can tell by the way they lie that those governments which take them away feel a little bit ashamed of themselves.

And I think it's fair to say that all this happened because of the American Revolution. America showed the world that a government based on the idea of liberty wasn't just a dreamy philosopher's fantasy—it could really work. Once the rest of the world saw that, many wanted it.

It's a great thing to have that kind of freedom. But I can't help pointing out that it's kind of a *negative* freedom. I don't mean "negative" as in "bad." I mean that it's all about what the government can't do to you, and not about what you *can* do.

That's by design, of course. Our Founding Fathers were dealing with a bunch of different states where people believed entirely different things in regards to religion, morals, and economics.

Actually, British subjects in England had a lot of freedom already. They had an elected Parliament to represent them, and while it was true that many people weren't considered good enough or important enough to vote for their representatives, they believed it was better than nothing. The people also had certain rights that couldn't be taken away.

But the British Parliament had treated the American colonies like property. Americans thought they had just as many rights as English people, but the king and Parliament didn't agree. Americans couldn't vote for representatives in Parliament, but Parliament could make any law it liked for the American colonies. It could tax Americans as much as it liked. And one thing that hasn't changed in two and a half centuries is that Americans really hate taxes.

So when it came time for us to write our Bill of Rights—the first ten amendments to our Constitution—we phrased it all in terms of what the government can't do.

"Congress shall make no law respecting an establishment of religion, or prohibiting the free exercise thereof; or abridging the freedom of speech, or of the press; or the right of the people peaceably to assemble, and to petition the Government for a redress of grievances." That's the First Amendment, which packs a lot of rights into one amendment. When people talk about freedom of religion, freedom of assembly, freedom of speech, freedom of the press, or freedom of petition, that's all in the First Amendment. (The humorist Dave Barry once said that the whole Bill of Rights could have been taken care of in one amendment: "Congress shall make no law." Period.)

Most of the other amendments in the Bill of Rights are negatively phrased, too. "No soldier shall, in time of peace, be quartered in any house without the consent of the owner, nor in time of war, but in a manner to be prescribed by law." (That was important, because all the colonists remembered the days when a British soldier might just show up at their door and say, "Guess what? I live with you now.") "The right of the People to be secure in their persons, houses, papers and effects, against unreasonable searches and seizures, shall not be violated. .... Excessive bail shall not be required, nor excessive fines imposed, nor cruel and unusual punishments inflicted."

These are all things the government can't do to you. And we say, "Hallelujah! That's great. But there's nothing here about what we *can* do." And that's the big difference between American-style freedom and Christian freedom. Christian freedom is all about what we *can* do.

I certainly want to be positive about American freedom, because I believe this is an amazing country, but I also want to help you understand that there's a much more important freedom than the freedom to be left alone by your government. This is the freedom to choose holiness, and this is a freedom no one can take away from us. It's true, people can make it harder. But they can't take away that freedom.

Think back to the martyrs under the Roman Empire. The Roman governors gave them a choice: renounce your Christian faith, or die torn to shreds by beasts in the arena. Well, I admit that makes it harder to choose holiness. It puts a little bit of an obstacle in the way. But the reason we remember the martyrs is that they made that choice anyway. They compared the short pain in the arena to the infinite bliss of Heaven, and they told the governors, "Nuts to you," (or words to that effect).

The might of the mightiest empire Europe ever saw couldn't take away a Christian's freedom to choose holiness. But much mightier forces are at work than that. Sure, they can't take your freedom to live holiness away, but they can make you fight for it.

## Satan and All His Pomps

You can't look around you without noticing that our society is growing more and more secular. By "secular," I really mean hostile to religion. There's a big difference between the religious freedom our Founding Fathers imagined and the anti-religious hostility we have to deal with today. The Founders imagined a world in which most people would be religious, but they would be different *kinds* of religious. It didn't matter whether we liked each other, as long as we agreed that the others had a right to exist. Of course people would bring their religious views along with them wherever they went, including into public life. The line you couldn't cross was clearly drawn: you couldn't force anybody to share your religious views. The government was friendly to all beliefs, because it wouldn't be allowed to promote any one of them.

Now, though, there's a strong pressure to keep religion out of public view completely, although I'll be fair and say that most of this hostility doesn't come from our government. For the most part—for the *most* part—the First Amendment is still working.

No, most of this hostility comes from society at large. Remember the ancient serpent I wrote about in the first chapter? He's at it again. Satan is attacking us in the way that's most effective for our age, spreading the message he brought to Adam and Eve: you can be wise on your own terms, without having to listen to all those silly rules. You can be smarter than God.

Make no mistake: this is war, and Satan has powerful armies.

When an adult is baptized into the Catholic Church, or when we renew the baptismal promises our parents made on our behalf, we renounce "Satan, and all his works, and all his empty show." An older English translation of the word we render as "empty show" is "pomps," and I like that, because I like saying "pomps." Pomps, pomps, pomps. It's a word that sounds a little ridiculous, and that helps me see that Satan's pomps are ridiculous in themselves. Satan tries to get us with spectacle and with arguments that sound convincing but don't have any substance. The only way to win the battle is to see through his pomps—to see them for the empty shells they are.

And this is a war, as I said. So I like to think of these pomps as Satan's generals in snappy uniforms covered with society's glittering, false ideologies. Our chief enemy in this battle is General Relativism. Of all Satan's pomps, he's the one who's been winning the most battles lately.

You've met General Relativism many times. You probably see him every day. The idea he constantly pushes is that there's no absolute truth. "You have your truth, and I have mine," he says. "You can't tell me what's 'true,' because 'truth' is a construct by the powerful meant to keep me from following my bliss."

"There really is no such thing as absolute truth, Jon," a friend of mine once told me. I thought about that for a moment, and then I replied, "Is that *absolutely true*?" I could hear a *clink* as one of General Relativism's medals fell to the ground.

That's the thing about relativism. When it attacks truth, it only destroys itself. If you think about it, it makes no sense at all to say that there's no absolute truth, because of course that statement in itself is supposed to be an absolute truth, which means the statement can't be true, which means . . . and we end up like Captain Kirk in the old *Star Trek* series, shorting out some villainous computer with loops of logic and watching it explode in a shower of cheap special effects.

So maybe you see through relativism in its most obvious form. "There is no absolute truth"—you understand why that doesn't make any sense. But General Relativism isn't through with you yet. Maybe you see through his logic. But he'll come at you through the fuzzy, warm platitudes of good feelings or the popular menu items of the day. They infect our thoughts without going through the logic circuits. The mantras this General and his minions live by are phrases like "You do you."

*You do you!*

I hear and see that popular phrase. It basically means

*do whatever you want, whenever you want, however you want to do it.* Of course, we all know this isn't the way life works. I'm even convinced that deep down, those who use phrases like this don't believe them. It sounds good; it may even be well intentioned, but it's no way to live. All you have to do is think about it for half a second and you realize why.

Remember when you were five and you wanted that giant cookie? Mom said no, but you didn't care. You wanted that giant cookie! So what did you do? You threw a tantrum. Mom said "maybe later," but you wanted the cookie right that moment. "After all," you thought, "what Mom *should* be saying to me is, 'Have whatever you want! Who cares what I think? You do you!' Who is she to tell me what's good for me? I should just take the cookie! And while I'm at it, I'm beginning to wonder why I spent all that time learning to use the toilet. And what's this 'school' thing they keep talking about anyway? And 'work'? Please! I don't do work. That's not me. As I see it, *you do you* means right here, right now, eating that cookie!"

So, you took the cookie when Mom wasn't looking. The cookie tasted good. The cookie was delicious! But was it worth it? Sure it *wasn't*. Why? Because Mom found out, and you didn't have another cookie for three weeks.

You can see the problem with this way of thinking a mile away, and hopefully you grew out of it. But some don't. Some still think it's their world and everyone is just walking through it. We're not. Life has certain rules to follow; your parents probably taught you many of them. Rewards and consequences are based on how we contribute to society and live our lives.

Like every one of Satan's wrong ideas, "you do you" starts with a real truth; that's what makes Satan so insidious. God made you an individual. There's no one else on earth like you. Even if you have an identical twin, you're different people, with different experiences that have formed you in different ways. That's all part of God's plan. Relativism scatters that plan. Relativism ignores the plan. Relativism destroys the plan God has for each of us—the plan to pursue holiness and become a saint.

Pursuing holiness is a journey; it's a vocation. Though the work isn't easy, God's grace is enough to get us there. When it gets hard, General Relativism gives the signal for an attack. "You can do whatever you want! It's easier that way! You're great just the way you are!" It's persuasive, because in a certain way, it's true. God *does* love you as you are. But God loves you enough that He wants you to keep going forward till you reach Heaven. And He's going to do everything He can to help you along the way.

Our society seems to be getting lonelier and lonelier. We have thousands of friends on Facebook, and yet we feel like there's nobody we can talk to. We have all these shiny electronics to make us happy, and yet so many feel miserable. Worst of all, we probably live in a world that's freer than it's ever been at any time in human history (although we still have a lot of work to do) and yet so many are bound by the wages of sin and death. So what do we do? I'll tell you. The Church will tell you: *pursue holiness and find the life you were meant to live.*

## Generals Malice and Envy

"For we ourselves were once foolish, disobedient, deluded, slaves to various desires and pleasures, living in malice and envy, hateful ourselves and hating one another" (Titus 3:3).

Oh, you can stop right there, Paul. Doesn't that describe the way too many of us Americans live our lives these days? We're enslaved to our desires and pleasures, and General Relativism, rubbing his hands together, is always there to tell us that this kind of slavery is "freedom," while Generals Malice and Envy tell us that we ought to have all the things we want.

You can't stop thinking about sex? Do what feels good! Be free!

You can't stop thinking about food? YOLO! (You Only Live Once.)

You can't stop coveting your neighbors' possessions? Look around you! You can buy all the same beautiful things on credit to look just like them, and all it will take is a low monthly payment of. . . . Well, how about we just don't even look at those low monthly payments, okay? I mean, it's a plastic card. It's not like its *real* money. Yet we're still living in malice and envy. We still look and see that those people over there have newer and better things: a more expensive car, a bigger house, a smarter smartphone.

So we end up isolating ourselves more. We go back to that phone, back to that TV, back to that store and try to console ourselves—with mindless entertainment, divisive politics, and store-bought stuff.

"Two in five Americans report that they sometimes or always feel their social relationships are not meaningful, and one in five says they feel lonely or socially isolated," says the United States government.[1] That has a real effect on us. It's not just that isolating ourselves puts us in a bad mood. "As a force in shaping our health, medical care pales in comparison with the circumstances of the communities in which we live. Few aspects of community are more powerful than is the degree of connectedness and social support for individuals." The statistics are sobering: "Loneliness is more dangerous than obesity and as damaging to health as smoking 15 cigarettes a day."

I don't think it's a coincidence that our general level of happiness has been going down here in the United States. People rate themselves as less happy with their lives now than they did a few years ago. We have more *stuff* now, but we're less happy.[2] So what do Generals Malice and Envy tell us?

General Malice tells us the reason we're not happy is because of *those* people over there. If they would only stop doing what they're doing—like, you know, being them—then it would solve our problems. General Envy tells us that what we need is *more stuff*. Those people over there have all the stuff! Why can't I have stuff? I want stuff too!

We hate one another, and we become hateful ourselves, just like Paul said. So we go on Facebook and post more comments about how we can't *believe* how much *those* people have. Then we look at the advertisements and buy more stuff. Generals Malice and Envy tell us those things will make us feel better, but they don't; we feel lonely and miserable.

## What Are We Really Looking For?

No matter how much Generals Relativism, Malice, and Envy try to persuade us that we want freedom to indulge in all our desires, to hate the people who are different from us, and to envy all their stuff, we have to see through them. We have to realize that what they're offering us isn't freedom at all.

We were made for the freedom not found in an ideology or a philosophy. We were made for a freedom that can't be found in all the "stuff" in the world. We were made for the freedom that is found in a person—Jesus the Christ.

So what we want to do is be freed from sin—from all those fake freedoms that Satan and his minions keep trying to push on us—and have the liberty to choose holiness.

Give me holiness or give me death! Actually, give me holiness because I'm going to get death no matter what.

Well, we're in luck! This is precisely what the Church exists to do; namely, to free us from sin and make us holy. Why holiness? Because holiness leads to Sanctity. Holiness leads to Heaven.

I'm going to end with something St. John Paul II said when he was visiting America.

The basic question before a democratic society is: 'how ought we to live together?' In seeking an answer to this question, can society exclude moral truth and moral reasoning? Can the Biblical wisdom which played such a formative part in the very founding of your country be excluded from that debate?

Would not doing so mean that America's founding documents no longer have any defining content, but are only the formal dressing of changing opinion? Would not doing so mean that tens of millions of Americans could no longer offer the contribution of their deepest convictions to the formation of public policy? Surely it is important for America that the moral truths which make freedom possible should be passed on to each new generation. Every generation of Americans needs to know that freedom consists not in doing what we like, but in having the right to do what we ought.[3]

Nailed it. That's what freedom—real Christian freedom—is. We're battling Satan and his generals on all fronts now, and we're going to win *if* we keep on fighting.

But I know human nature. We're not going to keep on fighting if we don't even understand what we're fighting for, which is why our most important weapon in this war is knowing God. We can't just know facts and arguments; we need a real and intimate love of God.

## FOR REFLECTION

Holiness leads to Sanctity. Holiness leads to Heaven.

*In what ways am I striving for Holiness in my daily life?*

## CHAPTER 5

# *To Know or to Know About*

I WANT TO KNOW GOD. I don't mean just know *about* God. I want to know God—to know who God the Father is, and what God the Father wants for me. I want to know His only Begotten Son, Jesus Christ, the second person of the Most Holy Trinity. I want to know the Paraclete, the Indweller of Believers, the Holy Spirit. Yes, I want to know the Triune God, three in one and one in three.

Now, don't get me wrong. I'm not saying I don't want to learn about God. In fact, I spend my life learning and writing and speaking about God. But more than any of those three things, I want to know God. And in knowing Him, I want to love Him with everything I have.

## Knowledge Is Good

I have to confess I'm a bit obsessive about theology. While my wife is reading Lord of the Rings for the 84th time, I'll be right next to her with that massive green book, the Catechism of the Catholic Church. Isn't that a little like reading the phone book? (she asks). No, not at all. It just fascinates me how the whole story of salvation is laid out in that book, how it all fits together, how there's an answer for every question you could think of about how to live your life. Okay, you can say it: I'm a Catechism nerd.

It's not just the Catechism, of course. I spend a lot of time in Scripture, because if you don't know Scripture, you don't have the foundation to build up any other knowledge of the faith. Also, the Bible is the most amazing book ever. I've said it before, but I'll say it again: every kind of story and every kind of literature is in that book. Poetry, philosophy, drama, adventure, comedy—it's all there.

I also love reading about the lives of the saints, and reading what the saints themselves wrote. Some of the best writers in history are on the list of Catholic saints. If you're looking for something good to read, you can just go down the list. The mystical experiences of Teresa of Avila have always fascinated me, and I'm sure you'll find something that really speaks to you among the thousands and thousands of books written by and about the saints.

I love reading about the history of the Church, too. It's inspiring, humbling, infuriating, and consoling all at the same time. When you actually know the history of the Church, you can see that the Holy Spirit really was guiding it. There's no other explanation. I mean, you read all about the heroes, and that's inspiring. But plenty of villains are in the history of the Church, too: bad popes, corrupt bishops, mobs with torches and pitchforks. But the Church never swerved from the true doctrine; that's the amazing thing. No matter how corrupt or misguided any individual member of the Church might have been, the Church has kept on the same path for just about 2000 years. I don't think you can account for that without a miracle.

So I'm not telling you not to learn *about* God and the Church; I'd never tell you that. For one thing, you'd stop buying my books. For another thing, the more you know about God and the Church, the better you know the way to Heaven.

### *Knowing God* Is Even Better

But over the years, I've come to realize that knowing about God isn't the same thing as *knowing God*; in fact, it's very different. The whole reason we learn about God is so that we can come to know God as He is. Yes, our learning should funnel us into knowing, so don't use what I'm about to say as an excuse not to study our incredible faith. In fact, studying the faith led many of the saints to deepen their relationship with God, and if the saints understood this, we should too.

But learning is part of the journey; our ultimate destination is knowing God personally. That personal acquaintance starts with building your relationship here, right now, with prayer. After all, as I'm fond of saying, faith without prayer is a hobby.

I don't think I learned how to actually pray until I was in seminary. It sounds strange, I know, because of course I learned to say prayers. I was raised a Catholic, and I learned many of the same prayers I'm teaching my own kids. I said my "Hail Marys" and "Bless us O Lords." But that real, honest relationship with Jesus just wasn't there growing up.

If you think I'm the model of what prayer should look like now, you're fooling yourself. Or I'm fooling you. I am *not* the model of what true intimacy with Christ is.

But like you, I try. And where I am now in my prayer life is a lot further than where I was even just a few years ago. I've seen real fruits born from my deepening prayer life, and that deepening comes from getting to know Christ better as a person—which in turn comes from knowing more *about* Christ from the Scriptures and from the writings of the saints.

It's strange, really. Sometimes I look back on my life and don't even know that guy. I've changed a lot. Sometimes I'm a little bit embarrassed by what I was back then. I thought I knew everything. I didn't. I thought I had all the answers. I don't. In fact, the more I know now, the more I know that I'm a mess. But I'm slowly changing.

No, I'm not changing on my own. God is changing me. As I said, He's certainly not done with me yet. I am still a knuckle-headed sinner in need of God's mercy. But I also know that this relationship with Christ is real, and there's just no other road for me than this.

And God knows us, too. Don't forget that God has had all the same human experiences we've had, only worse. Jesus Christ was completely human. It hurt when He hit his thumb with a hammer. It hurt when He stepped on a thorn (they have ferocious thorns in Palestine). It hurt much worse when His friend Lazarus died and his other friends were inconsolably sad. And I think it's pretty safe to say that nobody likes being crucified.

So we were made in God's image, which means that we have a built-in capacity to get to know God. And God has been one of us, which means that, even aside from the fact that He created us, He knows the human experience from the inside. We can have a relationship with God. And that's the whole point of our faith.

## The Crisis of the Presence of God

One of my favorite books of all time was written by a Catholic monk named Brother Lawrence of the Resurrection. We'll learn more about him soon, but the important thing to know is that he was a very simple man—simple in the sense of uncomplicated. He wasn't a trained theologian; he was just someone who got to know God very well.

The book is entitled *The Practice of the Presence of God*. Of all the books I've read on the spiritual life, this is most certainly in my top five. It's also one of the simplest and shortest books about the spiritual life I've ever read, which I think gives more credibility to it being so good. Half the book is a series of conversations with Brother Lawrence as remembered by one of his friends; the other half is a few letters he wrote.

In this book I found one of the most powerful lines I've ever read. He says, simply, "I cannot imagine how religious persons can live satisfied without the practice of the presence of God."

Now, notice that he doesn't say "persons." He says "*religious* persons." I can imagine how it would be possible to drift so far from God that you think you're perfectly fine without Him. You're not perfectly fine, of course, but I can imagine *thinking* you're perfectly fine. But that's not you, and that's not me. We're Christians. Most of my readers, obviously, will be Catholics, and most of you go to church regularly and do the things Catholics do.

Nevertheless, I think most of us are missing what Brother Lawrence called "the practice of the presence of God." I certainly was. I think it's a real problem, one that pervades the whole American Catholic Church. I'd even go so far as to say it's a crisis. Put simply, many Catholics don't know how to pray.

I'm not talking about, you know, the non-practicing Catholics out there. Lots of people call themselves Catholic but never show up at church, except maybe on Christmas and Easter, and then only if they have family with them. Those aren't the ones I'm worried about. I mean, not that I don't worry about them, but that's a whole separate problem. I'm talking about many of the "good" Catholics who sit in our pews every Sunday, and even many of the ones who go to daily Mass. I think many Catholics have never really learned to pray.

It's not their fault, honestly. I think many of the Church authorities and teachers have failed us in this pillar of faith. Many have just taken for granted that we can pursue holiness all on our own—that we all have our "own unique relationship with God." And they're not wrong about that. I want to make it very clear: we do have our own unique relationship with God, every one of us. But you can't just leave it at that. I can understand how they got to that point. They were reacting to a time when maybe we went too far in the other direction. They didn't want to be the ones who told Catholics just to shut up and do as they're told. They understood that liberty is very important. But we can't ever form a unique relationship with God if no one ever teaches us how to form a relationship in the first place.

Remember me at five years old, wanting the cookie? What if my parents had just decided I was perfect when I was five years old? What if they had stopped trying to teach me how to be a polite and useful member of grown-up society? I might have been happy about the cookie, for about a minute-and-a-half. I would not have grown up into a happy human being.

So I think we fail people when we say that each person has a unique relationship with God, and then just leave it at that. You have to learn *how* to have a relationship with God, just as a child who's five years old had to learn how to live in society without demanding a cookie every five minutes.

So that's why I'm spending so much time trying to make this careful distinction. Is there something unique to each persons relationship with God? Of course there is. That's why God made us all individuals instead of stamping us all out from the same mold.

But that doesn't mean we can leave people to figure it out on their own! We can't turn people loose and tell them to have a kind of "you do you" spiritual life. It's almost like we haven't learned from the past! Throughout the centuries, the Church has seen the consequences and even heresies when this sort of thinking happens. Think of the Protestant Reformation, for example. It started out with some real grievances and some important ideas. But as soon as people broke away from the Catholic Church and decided that "you do you" was the rule, they split, and split again, and split again, until thousands of Protestant sects were all fighting each other. That all comes from insisting, "I'm the only one who can tell me anything about my own relationship with God." No! You are the only one who can have that relationship with God. But, just as your parents taught you how to get along with other people, the Church is here to tell you how to start and deepen your relationship with God.

This is really what I'm doing when I'm giving parish missions around the country. No, I'm not giving them Jon Leonetti insights and tools. Those don't work, trust me. I'm giving the Church's tools and the saints' insights to better know God.

Over the past couple of generations, we've veered too far in the new-age me-generation direction. It's all about me. I'm who I am, and who I am is great.

That's our old enemy General Relativism with the most effective weapon in his whole arsenal. Like all the weapons the other side brings against us, these arguments work because they have some truth to them. I can't emphasize that truth enough. You *are* special. You *are* uniquely good. God made you to be you. General Relativism wants you to believe that he's the only one with that message, but he's lying.

Remember: God made you to be the person you *can* be, not to stop right where you are and decide that you're satisfied. You're still making you, right up to the day you die. Life is a pilgrimage, and you need to move in the right direction all the time. The direction you and I need to move in is the direction all of us were made to move in.

That's right. We're all in this together. It's a group effort. You can't do it alone.

Why?

Because you are not an island. We were all made to pursue holiness together. That's what the Church is about.

But if the secular models that are popular now are pushing us in the wrong direction, where can we find models to push us in the right direction?

They're all around us. That big green book I spoke about above (the catechism) is a good place to start. The Bible is even better. The lives, teachings, and wisdom of the saints have helped me tremendously. Add spiritual direction, surrounding yourself with friends, and pursuing holiness to the list . . . yeah, I could go on.

Why all these things? Because we know they actually work. They made saints. Remember that the canonized saints are people whom we know are in Heaven. We've found it out by the strongest possible proofs. So it only makes sense to look to them to show us the way to get there.

We can and should learn from one another and see the patterns in the spiritual life that have *worked* in making great saints, and will help us become holy too. If you think I'm leading up to a chapter with some saints in it, well . . . you know me pretty well.

**FOR REFLECTION**

We were made in God's image, which means that we have a built-in capacity to get to know God.

*What is one devotion in the Church you can make more time for?*

## CHAPTER 6

# Three Models for Deeper Prayer

NYONE WHO'S EVER READ MY BOOKS KNOWS ONE thing: I always have chapter(s) dedicated to the saints. Now, in most of my other books I concentrated more on the physical battles they overcame and deeply heroic acts they made. But the saints I've chosen here are three models for what's most important: deeper prayer.

After all, if we are going to pursue holiness, the first thing we need to look for is a right relationship with God, and that doesn't come to us until we open ourselves up to Him. Prayer goes two ways: we speak to God, but we also have to be ready for God to speak to us. That means being humble enough to let God have His way; we have to wait for Him to answer.

So here are three saints who'll help teach us about praying the right way. They're three very different kinds of people, but I think they all have this in common: they were humble and willing to listen.

We'll start with a nice lady who couldn't imagine why she was anybody special. But history has respectfully disagreed with her; she's remembered now as a Doctor of the Church.

## St. Teresa of Avila: A Model for Advancement

Perhaps you've heard me talk about St. Teresa of Avila. I never get tired of her. She was feisty and funny, real and dramatic. But she was also a mystic. It's a strange combination; she's like the most down-to-earth mystic you've ever heard of. Actually, though, I think a lot of the famous mystics were more down-to-earth than we think. These days, when we hear the word "mystic," we think of a guy sitting in the lotus position on top of a mountain with his eyes closed, at one with the Universe.

But that's not your typical Christian mystic. Your typical Christian mystic, in fact, is usually a down-to-earth person who happens to have amazing spiritual experiences sometimes. And St. Teresa is both one of the most mystical and one of the most down-to-earth Christians that's ever lived. To me, she embodies what it means to be *fully alive,* and yet she gave up what most people would think of as the good life to live in the deepest poverty.

Teresa of Avila was a noblewoman in Spain who decided to give up her life of luxury and become a Carmelite nun. But when she got to the convent, it seemed to her that she hadn't given up her life of luxury at all. The nuns lived in splendid buildings. They had society friends over to gossip all day. They went into town whenever they liked. They even wore shoes.

The Carmelites were an order that had been founded on Mount Carmel in the Holy Land during the Crusades. They had been dedicated to poverty and asceticism. But over the centuries, their rule had relaxed more and more. By the 1500s, the Carmelites, like a lot of other orders, were often living in luxury, or at least what would have seemed like luxury to those original Carmelites in the Holy Land. The luxury of monks and nuns was one of the weapons the new Protestants were using to bash the Catholic Church. What could one woman do about all that? What one woman could do was listen to the Gospel and pursue holiness.

"But seeing that I was a woman and a sinner, disabled from promoting as I desired the service of our Lord. . . . I resolved to do what little I could do; namely, follow the evangelical counsels with all the perfection I could."[4]

In 1560, Teresa met with a group of a dozen other nuns, and together they decided they were going to live by the ancient rule of the original Carmelites. Above all, they would live in poverty. They would own nothing, not even a pair of shoes. Jesus wore simple sandals, and that would be good enough for Teresa and her sisters.

The idea of going back to the life of luxury she had left filled Teresa with horror. "And if I could wish it with a good conscience, I would wish that the same day you build a costly house it may fall down and kill you all—I would wish it, and pray to God for it."[5]

The new order owned literally nothing, but somehow God provided. "And if sometimes there was not provision enough for all, all I had to do was say that only those who needed it most should partake of it, and each one considered herself not to be the most needy. And thus the food remained till God sent enough for all."[6]

But then came the villains of the story.

Now, we have to be clear here: the villains of the story weren't necessarily villains. It was a time when people divided themselves up into blocks, like today. Are you with us or against us? It was too easy to assume that someone who was protesting the corruption of the order must be against us. She must be just like those wicked Protestants. So the leaders of the Carmelite order stepped on Teresa's reform. The Spanish Inquisition even started to come after Teresa herself. (Nobody expected that!)

This is where Teresa was wiser than I would be. I'd get into arguments. I'd dig into my position. But Teresa . . . just obeyed. They told her to give up her public life, go into retirement, and keep quiet. So she did, and her obedience gave wiser leaders time to prevail. Just a few years later, the new order of "Discalced" ("shoeless") Carmelites was recognized by the Pope. Teresa lived to see almost three dozen monasteries and convents following her rule, and she also wrote some very important books. One of them was an autobiography, which is how I know something about her life. But her most important spiritual work is one known in English as *The Interior Castle*.

Teresa of Avila is hard to skim through and summarize because she didn't think in a linear fashion. She wrote things down as they came to her, and if she forgot about something a few pages prior, she'd just write it right in with an apology. "God help me! How I have wandered from my subject! I forget what I was speaking about, for my occupations and ill-health often force me to cease writing until some more suitable time. The sense will be very disconnected; as my memory is extremely bad and I have no time to read over what is written, even what I really understand is expressed very vaguely, at least I fear so."

But I think this same habit makes her an entertaining companion, because she seems like she's right here in the room with me saying, "Oh, and another thing about that thing I was talking about earlier. . . ." And if I look the slightest bit grumpy, she says, "Now, I'm just a poor old woman who doesn't know anything, and you're going to have to be patient with me."

And then I remember: Doctor of the Church. I can afford to be patient. Believe me; it's worth it, even if you're the sort who normally breezes through a book looking for the main points. You can't do that with anything written by St. Teresa; you have to spend time with the nice old lady who will make you wish she had been your grandmother.

*The Interior Castle* was recommended to me by my rector in college seminary, and it's one of those books I've never stopped reading. It's deep, yes, but I think it's one of the greatest books on Christian prayer ever written, for whatever my recommendation is worth.

According to people who knew St. Teresa, she didn't want to write *The Interior Castle*. The superior of her order almost had to force her to do it. Why? Like a saint, she was modest. So many great saints had written books—what was left for a poor woman to write?

The only reason she finally picked up the pen was the same reason she retired when she was told to retire: she had taken a vow of obedience, which meant she had to do what her superior told her to do. But she could still complain about it, in the gentlest and humblest way.

"Rarely has obedience laid upon me so difficult a task as this of writing about prayer; for one reason, because I do not feel that God has given me either the power or the desire for it, besides which, during the last three months I have suffered from noises and a great weakness in my head that have made it painful for me to write even on necessary business."

Even though she obeyed, Teresa had no idea she was writing what would be one of the great spiritual classics of all time. As far as she was concerned, she was writing just for the sisters—an idea her superior probably put in her head to make it easier for her to write what had to be written. "He who bids me write this, tells me that the nuns of these convents of our Lady of Carmel need someone to solve their difficulties about prayer: he thinks that women understand one another's language best and that my Sisters' affection for me would make them pay special attention to my words, therefore it is important for me to explain the subject clearly to them. Thus I am writing only to my Sisters; the idea that anyone else could benefit by what I say would be absurd."

But once she got started, she moved along at a furious pace. The same friend remembered seeing Teresa's hand run across the paper so fast it almost seemed supernatural. Once, when she walked in to deliver a message, Teresa told her to sit down "and let me write what our Lord has told me before I forget it," and scribbled furiously without stopping. If ever there was a blueprint of what the pursuit of holiness looks like, it's these seven mansions. That's what you'll find in *The Interior Castle:* concentric layers of "mansions," each one closer to God at the center.

## The Castle of the Soul

I thought of the soul as resembling a castle, formed of a single diamond or a very transparent crystal, and containing many rooms, just as in Heaven there are many mansions.... Let us imagine, as I said, that there are many rooms in this castle, of which some are above, some below, others at the side; in the center, in the very midst of them all, is the principal chamber in which God and the soul hold their most secret intercourse.

This beautiful castle is there in everyone, but strangely, many people never even try to get in. They're so used to living with the vermin and wild animals in the polluted land around the castle that they never think of trying to get in. The reason, Teresa says, is that they don't pray.

I was recently told by a great theologian that souls without prayer are like bodies, palsied and lame, having hands and feet they cannot use. Just so, there are souls so infirm and accustomed to think of nothing but earthly matters, that there seems no cure for them. It appears impossible for them to retire into their own hearts; accustomed as they are to be with the reptiles and other creatures which live outside the castle, they have come at last to imitate their habits. . . .

As far as I can understand, the gate by which to enter this castle is prayer and meditation.

Inside the castle are many mansions, just as there are in Heaven. But we can imagine them as arranged in rings around the center of the castle.

In the center of the castle is the keep—the stronghold where the soul experiences it's deepest union with God. The rest of the castle is arranged in rings around that keep. There are many, many rooms, but you can measure your progress through the seven concentric "mansions" arranged around the middle like the layers of an onion.

Oh, and before I describe these mansions, you should probably know that from here on, you're the main character in the story. It's your soul that has now entered the mansion.

### The First Mansion

When you first go in, St. Teresa says, a lot of the wild animals from outside the castle—meaning the bad thoughts and worldly attractions—come in with you, making it hard to concentrate on the beauty of the castle. Anyway, you're just in the basement. But still, it's a great thing just to have come into the castle in the first place. God has taken the first step of inviting you in, and you have taken the second in accepting His invitation. You've taken your first step.

Remember, though, just because you're inside the castle now doesn't mean you're safe. Yes, God is there, but the devil is there too. Teresa reminds you that the devil and his minions have infiltrated this castle. Demons are lurking in all the dark corners to keep you from progressing deeper in love and union with God. Of course, you won't let them though, because you know what's at stake.

### The Second Mansion

You have now made your way to the second mansion in the castle. You've made some progress. You've begun to pray regularly and with discipline, and you're aware that there is no greater prize in this world than deep prayer and union with God.

You still have trouble avoiding occasions of sin, it's true. But God is calling you through the words of preachers and good books. Teresa encourages you to keep at this for six months, a year, or even more. You're watching for the demons, because you know they're doing all they can to lead you backward instead of forward, and you trust God to bring good even out of your lapses.

If you keep on the right path, and turn back to God for forgiveness when you stray, you'll make it to the next room.

## The Third Mansion

The third mansion holds souls who are well on their way. "We may well call these souls blessed, for, as far as we can tell, unless they turn back on their course they are on the safe road to salvation." Great! You're home free now. "Now, my sisters, you see how important it is for them to conquer in their former struggles, for I am convinced that our Lord will henceforth never cease to keep them in security of conscience, which is no small boon."

But then she quickly adds, "I am wrong in saying 'security,' for there is no security in this life; understand that in such cases I always imply: 'If they do not cease to continue as they have begun.' What misery to live in this world! We are like men whose enemies are at the door, who must not lay aside their arms, even while sleeping or eating, and are always in dread lest the foe should enter the fortress by some breach in the walls."

So you've done well. You are continuing to allow God to speak and act in you. But you know you can't let your guard down, because the devil is still after you. He will never give up. But neither will God, and God is much, much more powerful than an evil creature. You've progressed well, but now you are likely to suffer bouts of spiritual dryness—the feeling that your prayers are having no effect. Perhaps you don't feel the presence of God like you used to, and life's trials feel heavier or more burdensome. But you know, in the deepest recess of your heart that God has not, and will never, abandon you. Trials only serve to school you in detachment from the things of this world. After all, that's the goal of the spiritual life. So, right now, you keep asking God for humility. Of course, don't expect to get out of your dry path right away. Just keep going, with your eyes fixed on Christ, and you'll get to the fourth mansion.

### The Fourth Mansion

It took a long time to get here. Now you're in a very beautiful part of the castle, and the things you experience can't be put into words. Teresa says that the vermin from outside rarely come into this part of the castle, and when they do, they do more good than harm, because those temptations help keep you humble.

That doesn't mean you won't have difficulties; life is filled with them. St. Teresa herself suffered from an epic case of tinnitus, hearing a constant, loud rushing sound and twittering birds in her head. But there were times when she felt God's peace pouring into her, and everything was quiet, and you will too. That prayer of quiet is the kind of experience you can expect if you make it to the fourth mansion.

### The Fifth Mansion

To make it to the fifth mansion, you need to be ready to give everything to God. Then you're ready to go beyond the prayer of quiet to what Teresa calls the prayer of union. This union never lasts very long—less than half an hour, Teresa says. But it will leave you with the urge to go even deeper into the castle, to progress further in your spiritual development and to want to lead others to that same state of blissful union with God as well.

When someone asks you what this union with God is like, you have trouble finding the words. But you know that this love you feel for God is not, and will never be, of human effort. This is God acting in your soul. While this is happening, the devil can't harm you, and the little vermin—your distracting desires and temptations—can't get in as far as the fifth mansion.

You're like the silkworm that has spun its cocoon: the worldly you dies like the worm, and you emerge as a beautiful white moth.

However, you can still fall from that state. If you stray from the path, figuring you've got it made now, you can be as short-lived as that little white butterfly. The way we keep on the right path is through love of God and love of neighbor. So watch out for the little things. The devil can't get between us and God in those moments of union, but he can attack us in the little things, the things that seem like they don't matter.

But if you do that, it seems like you've made it, right? Well, no.

### The Sixth Mansion

In the sixth mansion, you're determined to be united to the Lord. Yes, troubles within and without continue to assail you. You may have serious illnesses and sufferings, as Teresa did. Or you may not. Teresa warns you that Satan—who really doesn't want you to get any further into the castle—will still assault you with doubts, trying to make you think God has rejected you at different times of your life. But as consolation, God sends even more graces, coming to you when you're not even thinking about Him. You may even experience a kind of ecstasy or trance state at times as well. Some of these experiences are unsettling at first, and you're going to need courage to accept these rewards.

## *The Seventh Mansion*

Finally, escaping Satan's wiles, you reach the seventh mansion, and here the three persons of the Trinity are revealed.

That doesn't mean they're revealed all the time. If you had that vision all the time, you couldn't get anything else done. Plus you still have a job here: you're meant to be serving God's people around you. This new closeness to God, whom you found at the center of your own soul, makes you a dynamo of charity.

This is the big difference between Christian mystics and the cartoon mystics who sit on mountains with their eyes closed. Christians come back from those mystical experiences with new power to help their sisters and brothers around them. Now, as St. Teresa points out, this is just a general overview of that interior castle. There are so many beautiful rooms—so many amazing spiritual experiences to be had—that you'll never tire of the place.

"Although I have only mentioned seven mansions, yet each one contains many more rooms, above, below, and around it, with fair gardens, fountains, and labyrinths, besides other things so delightful that you will wish to consume yourself in praising the great God for them, who has created the soul in His own image and likeness."

I can't leave St. Teresa without harping on one of my favorite themes. St. Edith Stein, who had been an atheist, was converted to Catholicism by reading the works of St. Teresa of Avila. She entered St. Teresa's order, the Discalced Carmelites, and took the name Teresa Benedicta of the Cross. That's what I'm always talking about: the saints make saints.

*So, what can we learn from St. Teresa? God is calling us to deeper union with Him. It will happen on His time and His terms, we simply, each step of the way, allow Him to lead us further into the castle of Divine love.*

## Brother Lawrence of the Resurrection: The Model of Simplicity

Our next example actually isn't a canonized saint. He may never be canonized, for all I know, and that would be fine by him. All he ever cared about was having a straightforward relationship with God.

Brother Lawrence of the Resurrection, whose original name was Nicolas Herman, was born in about 1614—his parents were so poor they couldn't afford an exact birth date. There was only one real growth industry in Europe at the time, and that was war, specifically the Thirty Years' War, which was basically a war between Catholics and Protestants. It was one of the most horrible wars in history. Millions of people died—either in battle or from disease and hunger—and it seemed to go on forever. As a soldier, young Nicolas saw the worst of it. A leg wound made him lame for life, so he was no longer useful in the army.

It was while he was an ordinary young soldier that he had a profound spiritual experience—profound, but simple, like everything else about him.

It was winter, and he saw a tree. The tree had no leaves—because, you know, it was winter. That was all he saw. But it was what the tree made him think of that was important. In a little while it would be spring, and the leaves would start to come out. Then there would be flowers. Then there would be fruit. It always happens: winter gives way to spring. What seems to be dead comes to life again.

More than four decades later he remembered the experience as the turning point of his life. Suddenly, he had known how great the power of God was, and how much God cared for the humblest parts of His creation, and "this view had perfectly set him loose from the world, and kindled in him such a love for God that he could not tell whether it had increased during the more than forty years he had lived since."

After the army he had to find a job, so he became a footman, a servant whose job was to be something like a waiter at the master's table. He handled the dishes and glasses, but he asserted that "he was a great awkward fellow who broke everything." So not only was he a humble servant, but he was also bad at it.

He felt very guilty about it, too, so he decided to become a monk (that was when he took the name Lawrence of the Resurrection), because he thought that monastery life would be unpleasant, so he'd be punished for his inadequacies. Imagine his disappointment when he found he actually liked the monastery! In fact it was a monastery of Discalced Carmelites—St. Teresa's order—so life was bare and simple. But it was comfortable and pleasant. The monastery put him in the kitchen (he didn't really like the kitchen, but he found that God made him very contented with his work), and that was where he stayed until, when he was old, his leg wouldn't hold him up in the kitchen anymore. Then he was assigned to work on sandals, which Discalced Carmelites always need.

When he decided to give his life to God, Lawrence read some very well-written books that told him all about how to develop his spiritual life. However, he ignored all their advice. Oops. Well, I hope I'm doing better. "Having found in many books different methods of going to God, and divers practices of the spiritual life, I thought this would serve rather to puzzle me than facilitate what I sought after, which was nothing but how to become wholly God's." I think that's the big secret Brother Lawrence discovered: *you don't have to make this complicated.* God meets us where we are. And He works right there with what we've got. It's a simple friendship he desires.

Brother Lawrence was never very well educated, and he certainly didn't have splendid spiritual visions like St. Teresa. But he found the way to be in God's presence that suited him and other simple people (like me): just to have a conversation with God. As he said, "we should establish ourselves in a sense of God's presence by continually conversing with Him . . . it was a shameful thing to quit his conversation to think of trifles and fooleries."

Brother Lawrence wrote down some advice for Christians that was only found after he had died: "All things are possible to one who believes, and even more to one who hopes, and even more to one who loves, and even more to one who practices and perseveres in those three virtues; all who are baptized, believing as they ought to believe, have taken the first step along the road to perfection, and will be perfect so long as they persevere in the following maxims."

But it's not going to be easy all the time. For ten years, Brother Lawrence suffered from doubt. Not doubt that God existed, but doubt about whether he was doing enough for God. Was he really worthy of all the gifts God had for him? Wasn't he being presumptuous to imagine that God would actually care enough about him to have anything to do with him? Finally, after ten years, something wonderful happened. He gave up. He stopped wanting to be through with his troubles. He surrendered to God.

"But then, when I no longer wanted anything but to end my days in these troubles and worries (which had not diminished the trust I had in God one bit, and which only served to increase my faith), I suddenly found myself changed, and my soul, which until then had been constantly troubled, felt a profound inner peace, as if it was in its center, and in a place of rest."

When it gets hard is when we have to remember that even our suffering is a good thing, because it teaches us to rely on God. "We must believe without doubt that it is advantageous to us, and agreeable to God, to sacrifice ourselves to Him every day; that it is normal for His divine Providence to abandon us to all sorts of conditions, to suffer all sorts of pains, miseries, and temptations for the love of God, as long as He pleases, since without this submission of the heart and mind to the will of God, devotion and perfection cannot subsist."

The point is that you still keep up the conversation with God. It's not complicated. You have friends who stick with you in good times and bad; God wants to be that kind of friend to you.

Remember what Jesus said to his disciples: "You are my friends if you do what I command you. I no longer call you slaves, because a slave does not know what his master is doing. I have called you friends, because I have told you everything I have heard from my Father" (John 15:14–15).

That doesn't mean every one of us will experience what Brother Lawrence felt and experienced here in prayer, but he can teach us to stop overcomplicating the prayer life. He can teach us that no matter how insignificant we think we are, God desires all of us to swim the deep waters of prayer and love of Him.

I should point out that *The Practice of the Presence of God* is one of the few spiritual books that is just as popular among Protestants as among Catholics. So you can recommend it to your Protestant friends, and they'll probably love it. And maybe they'll pick up something they've been missing. Who knows?

*So, what can we learn from Brother Lawrence? In one word: simplicity. God isn't asking for anything complicated from us. What He wants is simple—a real friendship. Simple isn't the same as easy: my wife can tell you that being my spouse isn't always easy. But we get ourselves in trouble when we overthink it, and we stay out of trouble when we keep it simple. If all else fails, just let go and let God take over.*

## The Silence of St. Joseph

St. Joseph certainly has a pivotal place in history. He had to be a father to God incarnate. And I thought it was hard just raising ordinary, brilliant and amazing children like mine! It's striking that Joseph never says anything in the Bible. ("That's what makes him such an ideal husband," says somebody close to me whom I won't name right now.) But it's true. There's not a single word directly attributed to Joseph in any of the Gospels.

Why not?

It can't be because he was actually mute—I'm sure the Gospel writers would have told us something so extraordinary. They told us when it happened to Zechariah, the father of John the Baptist (see Luke 1:20). Nevertheless, we don't get any direct quotations from Joseph.

Yet Joseph seems to have been in constant communication with the divine. When Jesus was conceived, an angel told Joseph about it in a dream. When Herod was trying to kill the child Jesus, an angel warned Joseph. When it was safe to come back from Egypt, an angel told Joseph again. Then, once he got to Judea, Joseph had another dream warning him to leave Judea for Galilee. So we never hear Joseph saying anything, but we're told that he heard the voice of God four times.

I think that's our answer. I think we're supposed to *notice* that he's not talking, so we'll realize that he's *lis-*

*tening.* Silence is where we find God. We have to learn that lesson over and over again. We think of God as big and powerful—and He is, of course. And we think of big and powerful things as noisy. But really big and powerful things aren't noisy at all, when you think about it. Nothing in our solar system is as big and powerful as the sun, but you don't hear a thing from the sun. The galaxy is unimaginably bigger than the sun, but if you go out into the darkest dark night and look up at the Milky Way, you hear nothing.

Remember Elijah's experience? He probably thought of God the same way most people do—big, powerful, and loud. Certainly he'd seen some spectacular demonstrations of God's power, like when God sent fire down from Heaven to light the sacrifice and win the contest with the prophets of Baal (see 1 Kings 18).

But God decided to show Elijah—and us through Elijah—that the spectacle wasn't really God. On the very same mountain where Israel had received the Ten Commandments centuries earlier, God came to Elijah. You remember the story: it begins with a lot of special effects.

"There was a strong and violent wind rending the mountains and crushing rocks before the Lord," the text says. And, yes, it showed God's power—"but the Lord was not in the wind," the writer continues.

Then, "after the wind, an earthquake—but the Lord was not in the earthquake."

We're not done yet. Next came a fire—"but the Lord was not in the fire."

And finally, now that we've had all those special effects that Cecil B. De Mille would have loved, "after the fire, a light silent sound."

The noise is over. The light show is done. The earth has stopped shaking, and the tornado has passed. Now Elijah really has to *listen* to hear God in the silence. This is one of the most profound moments in the whole Old Testament.

Joseph's encounters with God also came in silence— the silence of the night, when he was asleep. Sometimes it pays to shut up and listen to what God wants to say. More than that, sometimes talking can do more harm than good.

What would their marriage have been like if Joseph had given Mary a stern lecture when he found out she was pregnant? How about if he hit the roof and said a lot of things he couldn't take back? But that wasn't Joseph. Even if he thought she was guilty, he was going to "divorce her quietly" (Matthew 1:19). Then, when he heard from the angel that the child was conceived through the Holy Spirit, he didn't have a lot of damage to repair.

Silence is also a good time to gather strength for the mission. Retreating to silence can prepare us for the moments we need to get to work.

I like to think Joseph gained strength in his silence.

It wasn't going to be easy to be the adoptive father of the Messiah. In fact, some of the Church Fathers suggested that Joseph wasn't thinking of divorcing Mary because he suspected her of adultery. Maybe he knew exactly what was going on, they said, and he was terrified to be so close to so much holiness.

But he didn't do anything right away. Instead, he listened to the angel's voice in the silence, and that gave God the chance to let him in on the plan—the plan that included him.

The plan was going to be hard and dangerous. But those visits from the angel in the silence of the night must have given Joseph a lot of strength. When he got to work, he was up to the task of protecting his family from every danger—even crazy King Herod.

Maybe we need to imitate St. Joseph more often. If we think our prayers aren't being answered, maybe it's just because we won't shut up and listen for a while. We have an innate need for silence—sacred silence—burning inside us. God gave us that need, because He made us to be His friends, and silence is where He can come to us. The need is all the more desperate now, because our world gets noisier and noisier. How many houses have you been in where the TV is literally never off? When was the last time you weren't listening to something in the background: music, TV, radio, audiobook, YouTube?

Find a way to make room for silence. Find a place

that's quiet—an empty room, a spot in the woods, a garden. Maybe your parish church! There's a reason most Catholic churches are open for prayer. Once you've found that place, remember what God said: "Be still and know that I am God" (Psalm 46:11).

Prayer is a conversation. I'm sure St. Joseph had things to say to God. When he learned that he was going to be the adoptive father of the Messiah, I'll bet he had a *lot* to say to God. But what was really important was that he stopped talking long enough to give God the chance to answer him in the silence.

*So, what can we learn from St. Joseph? Meet God in silence. Holiness does not happen in the noise, but in the silence of grace, where we conform to God, not in the ways of the world of loud chaos, but in the peaceful and gentle breeze of God in silence.*

**FOR REFLECTION**

We have an innate need for silence – sacred silence – burning inside us.

*How can I make more room for moments of sacred silence in my day?*

## CHAPTER 7

# *Backyard Missionary*

ALL RIGHT, SO WE'VE SEEN HOW THE SAINTS BUILT up their relationships with God. Each saint has a unique way of doing it, and each saint built up a unique relationship with God.

See! You do you! It works!

Well, not quite.

Every saint is unique, but they all have things in common, too. And, as I've said before (and I'll say it again), the big one is prayer. Prayer is the foundation of your unique relationship with God.

So you need to know what the Church asks of you and from her you will discover your own unique relationship with God. But I won't go over all that again, because it's time to move on to another important thing the saints all had in common. All of them had a deep connection with God, but they also knew that God gave them the spiritual gifts they had so that they could go out and share them with the rest of His people.

You've met God in the keep of your interior castle? That's wonderful! But you're not done. Now you have to bring that experience to the people who haven't had it. After all, you want everyone in the world to hear the gospel and pursue holiness.

So yes, it is your job. You are your brother's keeper. Who knew you were meant to be a missionary all along?

## Not Your *Normal* Missionary

I know there are people who devote their lives to being missionaries. Maybe your parish supports some of them. Maybe you take up a collection for the missionaries far away, to help keep them far away. Great! There's nothing wrong with that. Those missionaries are doing good work, bringing the Gospel to people who don't have a chance to hear it. But when you leave the church, you walk right out into a secular world that seldom has a chance to hear the Gospel. Guess what? That's your mission field!

What did Jesus tell his disciples just before he left them? I'll give you a hint. He didn't tell them to stay in the upper room and pray and then say, "Mission accomplished!" No, He was very explicit about what they had to do. "All power in Heaven and on earth has been given to me. Go, therefore, and make disciples of all nations, baptizing them in the name of the Father, and of the Son, and of the Holy Spirit, teaching them to observe all that I have commanded you" (Matthew 28:19–20). And again in Acts, just before He ascended, "But you will receive power when the holy Spirit comes upon you, and you will be my witnesses in Jerusalem, throughout Judea and Samaria, and to the ends of the earth" (Acts 1:8).

Yes, they would feel the power of the Holy Spirit coming to them. But there was a reason for that gift. It was so that they could take the message to the ends of the earth. Yeah, that's gonna be work. But we're not left alone to deal with it by ourselves. "And behold, I am with you always, until the end of the age" (Matthew 28:20).

That's why St. Teresa found God living in the middle of the castle of her soul. He doesn't live in a remote palace somewhere on a mountain. He comes with us wherever we go, and it's only because we're so distracted by the things of this world that we don't sense that all the time. But once we are in touch with that power, everything is different. It's like we have a nuclear generator with us all the time. With all that power to spare, you'll find that being a missionary isn't an option. You just have to do it. That's why Jesus didn't just tell us that it might be nice if we went out and spread the Gospel. He commanded it. Yes, that message is meant for us, too, not just the eleven remaining disciples.

"But I'm not a preacher!" That's what I hear you saying. (Alexa tells me everything.) Well, a lot of us aren't preachers. You don't have to love hearing yourself talk as much as I do. There are so many ways to be a saint! There's a way for me, and there's a way for you. You and I both have to find a way to follow that commandment to make disciples of all nations, but your way may be completely different from my way. The important thing is that we are pursuing holiness and want to help others pursue holiness as well.

In 1993, St. John Paul II was in Denver for World Youth Day. (He wasn't a canonized saint yet, of course, because, as I mentioned before, you have to be dead first to get into the canon.) I don't know how many people showed up to see him. Conservative estimates put the numbers somewhere in the low zillions. It was a young audience, of course—that's what World Youth Day is about. To all those young people with the rest of their lives ahead of them, St. John Paul spoke what I believe to be some of the most powerful words of his pontificate:

At this stage of history, the liberating message of the *Gospel of Life* has been put into your hands. And the mission of proclaiming it to the ends of the earth is now passing to your generation. Like the great Apostle Paul, you too must feel the full urgency of the task: "Woe to me if I do not evangelize" (1 Corinthians 9:16). *Woe to you if you do not succeed in defending life.* The Church needs your energies, your enthusiasm, your youthful ideals, in order to make the Gospel of Life penetrate the fabric of society, transforming people's hearts and the structures of society *in order to create a civilization of true justice and love.* Now more than ever, in a world that is often without light and without the courage of noble ideals, *people need the fresh, vital spirituality of the Gospel.*[7]

I'll bet many of the people who were there that day are still going to Mass every week, if not every day. You don't forget seeing one of history's great saints in person. But not everyone was there, and the numbers at Mass have been dwindling. In the 1950s, about three-quarters of Catholics went to Mass every week. Already, by the time St. John Paul was speaking to those young people in Denver, the number was down to 50%. Now, it's more like a third, and that's a third of the people who *identify* as Catholics.

The number of self-identified Catholics has been dropping as a percentage of the American population, too.[8] The Archdiocese of Philadelphia, which is a typical metropolitan area in this country, has seen its Mass attendance drop to less than half what it was in 1990. I don't remember 1990. But I was alive in 1990. This is a staggering drop.[9]

Okay, so that's a downer. We're losing members, which doesn't mean a thing in the big picture, because the big picture is that we're losing; *souls.*

But I choose to see the upside. How lucky we are! We don't have to cross the Pacific to New Guinea, or hack our way through some Amazon jungle, or trudge across the burning sands of the Sahara, just to find somewhere to spread the Gospel. Are you looking for the proper field for your missionary endeavors? Listen to Jesus, because He usually knows what He's talking about: "I tell you, look up and see the fields ripe for the harvest" (John 4:35).

Jesus said, "You will be my witnesses in Jerusalem, throughout Judea and Samaria, and to the ends of the earth." And you don't have to go to the ends of the earth to preach the Gospel when Judea and Samaria need your preaching right now. Judea and Samaria were the disciples' own back yard, and when the Christian movement started, they were as ignorant of the Gospel as the rest of the world.

Now, don't get me wrong. It's great to be a missionary in some faraway land. We need them. We probably wouldn't know the gospel without them. Think of Francis Xavier, who went to India and ended up all the way over in Japan, just because he couldn't stand the idea that there were people over there who hadn't heard the Gospel. He founded a Catholic Church in Japan that's still there today, and that has survived literally centuries of persecution and been driven underground like the ancient Roman Christians.

Or go way back to the Dark Ages, when most of the Germans were still pagans, and the bold English missionary St. Boniface went through the Germanic lands founding churches everywhere he went. It was dangerous work, and he ended up a martyr. But the world remembers him as the apostle of the Germans.

Or think of Mother Teresa. We call her St. Teresa of Calcutta, but she was actually a nice Albanian lady who ended up in India because it was where people needed her. She spent her life in some of the poorest and most crowded slums on earth, ministering to the poor and dying, spreading the Gospel by showing what it looked like in action. The whole world knew her by the time she died, and the whole world knew what it looks like when Christians really get to work.

So if that's your calling, go and do it. Be the missionary you were called to be. And if you think of it, bring back some Indian food for me. But maybe it's not your calling. Maybe your calling is to be a bank teller. Maybe you're meant to be an electrician, or a carpenter. Seems to me there was somebody famous in our faith who was a carpenter. It'll come to me in a moment.

The point is that being a plumber or a hairstylist or a cashier doesn't mean you're not a missionary. It just means you know where your mission field is. It's the world you live in every day. You're an evangelist in your own neighborhood, in your own hair salon, in your own little store. And you already know how to be an evangelist. Don't think so? I think you know how, but you just haven't thought about it yet.

## The Pizza Is Divine

The best pizza I've ever had doesn't come from one of those expensive artisan-pizza shops. It doesn't come from some famous pizzeria with an Italian name and people tossing crusts into the air like dough-juggling ballet dancers. No, the best pizza in the world comes from the gas station down the street from me.

Let me tell you about this pizza. Everything they do is right. The ingredients are perfect—I don't know where they get them, but the cheese melts just the way pizza cheese should melt, the pepperoni is better than anything I ever manage to get at the store, the sauce is always fresh, and the crust—oh, I could write poems about that crust. They would be bad poems, because I'm not as good at poems as I think I am (says my wife). Besides, they'd be about pizza crust. But I could write them.

Now, you see what's going on here? I'm *evangelizing* for my favorite gas station pizza. I don't know a lot of technical terms about pizza baking, or about the chemical processes that make a crust turn out perfect. But I find words to describe my experience. I tell everyone about this pizza; you can't shut me up about it.

I evangelize the same way when I see a movie I really love. I want everyone to see that movie and love it as much as I did. Why? Because it moved me, and I want it to do the same for others. The experience means more to me if other people share it, and I feel as though people I care about are missing something important if they don't have that wonderful experience.

I evangelize the Chicago Cubs too. (That used to be a hard job until a few years ago.) I share stories with my kids of how I came to love the Cubs, and I hope they do as well. I know a baseball team might not be important in the grand scheme of things. Okay, *intellectually* I know a baseball team might not be important in the grand scheme of things, but try telling my *heart* that. You probably do the same thing for your favorite sports teams, and you probably feel the same way: you want everyone else to feel the intense loyalty and attachment that you feel.

The point is that I just naturally share the things I really care about, and if all those things are important enough for me to evangelize about, how much more so is Jesus and the Church?

We often think of evangelizing as the job of our parish priest or the director of religious education. After all, they're the ones on the payroll. So they should be the ones proclaiming the good news of the gospel, right? I'll sit back and observe.

But it's not just their job. It's yours as well. Every one of us has been called in a unique way to proclaim the Gospel. Remember, God made *you* for a reason. If you're a priest, that's great. If you're not a priest, that's also great. The world needs every kind of person, every profession. And God needs us *all* to be evangelists.

The priest evangelizes from the front of the church. The director of religious education makes her contribution in the classroom. But you—you evangelize in your own back yard. No, I'm not asking you to get a bullhorn and stand in the middle of the street, although I do know people who have been very successful as street evangelist's. Hey, if that's your thing—go for it. (By the way, they don't use bullhorns. They use a friendly smile and a lot of patience.) But you don't have to stand on street corners, because—trust me—wherever you are, the people who need evangelizing will come to you. So then what do you do? Then you remember this book, because I'm about to give you some sure-fire techniques. (Spread the Gospel with these Six Weird Tricks!) These are simple, effective, everyday ways of being a missionary for Jesus, capturing hearts in moments and life-changing encounters, and it all starts at home.

## Home Base

Every missionary has a home base, right? So do you. It's called your home. The things in your home are expressions of who you are. Now I don't know what your house is like, but I have kids, so mine is full of chaos. We do a pretty good job of keeping it presentable, all things considered, and you can tell right away that a Catholic family lives here.

In my house, we have crucifixes, statues of saints, and Catholic books everywhere. Some of my friends have joked with me that there's really no need to go to the Vatican when they can just come over to my place for dinner. Now, before you think I'm asking you to take down the picture of grandma and hang a picture of St. Margaret of Scotland (she was the first one that came to mind here so I went with it), I'm not. You don't need to turn your home into the Sistine Chapel. But I do hope there are things of God on display somewhere: perhaps a crucifix in the hallway or by the door when people enter, a beautiful image of Our Lady in the family room or, a Bible on the coffee table.

Why is that important? Because these things can go a long way in evangelizing others, and you don't even have to say a word. Most of the people visiting your house, at least the ones who get far enough in to see what you have on your walls, probably already like you. Now they know what's important to you. They know that your faith is a big part of what makes you—the person they like, remember—who you are. So that's our first little evangelizing trick. Make your home an obviously Catholic place.

It's really simple and easy, but you'd be surprised how much it can do. I get asked questions all the time about evangelization. I hear from the father whose daughter has left the faith who wants to know how to get her back. Or I hear from the mother who thinks her son is falling in with the wrong crowd and doesn't care about the Church anymore. Others tell me they don't feel like they know enough to talk about the faith. Some tell me they're just plain embarrassed and don't want to be looked at as some sort of freak.

Are you one of those people? Then this is where you can start. Just make sure a few things in your house remind you—and anyone who walks in—of God. It's simple. It's easy. And believe me, the people you most want to be changed, the people you'd really like to lead on the road to holiness—they'll take notice.

## Taking Your Show on the Road

So you've made your home into a Catholic home. People who visit can see that your faith is important to you, and so can you, which I think will make a big difference in your own faith. That's a great first step. You've established your missionary home base. But you can't stay home all day. You've got a project due by 5:00pm today and a working lunch at 1:00pm that will eat into the time for your project. You've got to get to work! After that, you have groceries to buy, and you should probably stop at the hardware store and get a washer, because the faucet in the bathroom was dripping all night. Also, don't forget to make an appointment with the plumber to fix what you're going to do to the faucet when you try to put the washer in.

Yes, you have places to go and things to do, but if you think you can leave your missionary status on the hall tree at home, think again. You're a missionary at work. You're a missionary in the hardware store. Your job is to change hearts wherever you go.

Maybe it sounds scary, but this is what God is in the business of doing: changing hearts. If we're going to pursue holiness, we need to be in that business as well. After all, what's more important than that?

Again, it doesn't mean you have to go out and bang on doors or stand on street corners. You can if you want, but you don't have too. Think of Brother Lawrence. He just worked in the kitchen, or sat and made sandals, and people happened to notice that he had something they wanted. Just through ordinary conversations, he changed lives. People began to visit the monastery and ask to talk to the guy in the kitchen.

Or think of St. Thérèse of Lisieux, the "Little Flower." She lived her faith in the "little way," the way of simplicity and humility. She was never made a great leader; she never traveled around giving inspiring speeches; she never stood in the market and badgered people about their faith. But she lived as Christian a life as she knew how to live, and her sisters noticed. Once again, people sought her out. She insisted that she didn't have anything very complicated to say, but now she's a Doctor of the Church, which teaches us that simplicity is sometimes the height of wisdom.

So you don't need to be deeply educated. I do think the more you know about the faith the better, but God loves simple faith and simple love, and you don't have to be an extrovert to be a missionary. If you're living the Christian life, people will notice. Then you find your opportunities, one at a time, to explain how you got what they obviously want—no preaching in front of hundreds of people required.

But as I said before, for this to work, you have to constantly seek to deepen your faith and love for Jesus. There is a reason I placed the previous chapter, the one with the three great models of spirituality, in front of this one. You know the adage: you can't give what you don't have. This is most especially true in the spiritual life.

Now, don't get me wrong, you do not need to ascend to the depths of Teresa of Avila or Brother Lawrence when you set out. But you must be trying, seeking, wanting, and praying for the next phase to take place.

Now I have one more model of faith to present to you in the next chapter, and the next chapter is also the last, so if you've read a couple of my other books, you already know who she is.

**FOR REFLECTION**

You're a missionary at work. You're a missionary in the hardware store. Your job is to change hearts wherever you go.

*What is one way I can be a better missionary for Jesus in my daily life?*

## THE MAGNIFICAT

*My soul Magnifies the Lord*
*And my spirit rejoices in God my Savior*
*Because He has regarded the lowliness of His*
*handmaid*
*For behold, henceforth all generations shall call me*
*blessed*
*Because He who is mighty has done great things for*
*me, and holy is His name*
*And His mercy is from generation to generation on*
*those who fear Him*
*He has shown might with His arm;*
*He has scattered the proud in the conceit of their*
*heart;*
*He has put down the mighty from their thrones, and*
*has exalted the lowly.*
*He has filled the hungry with good things and the*
*rich He has sent away empty.*
*He has given help to Israel, his servant, mindful of*
*His mercy*
*Even as he spoke to our fathers, to Abraham and to*
*his posterity forever.*

## CHAPTER 8

# Holiness Personified

**W**HAT DOES HOLINESS LOOK LIKE PERSONIFIED?
Mother Mary.

You knew I was coming to the chapter about Mary, and now here it is. Mary is the model for everything we've been talking about, and this book wouldn't work without a chapter dedicated to her. She lived the holy life to the fullest. She's the ultimate example of Christian freedom: she *chose* to say, "Behold, I am the handmaid of the Lord. May it be done to me according to your word" (Luke 1:38). She not only pursued holiness herself, but she taught all of us how to do it—by following her Son. "Do whatever He tells you," she said to the people serving at the wedding at Cana (John 2:5), and nobody ever got better advice than that. To make her ready for her pivotal role in the salvation of everybody, Jesus gave His mother a gift nobody else in history ever had. She was born without sin.

## The Immaculate Conception

Everyone, Catholic or non-Catholic, hears the words "Immaculate Conception" and knows that has something to do with Mary. But lots of people misunderstand the idea of the Immaculate Conception. I think you'll find that even a lot of Catholics mix up the Immaculate Conception and the Virgin Birth. In fact, I *know* you'll find that a lot of Catholics mix them up, because I just looked on the Internet.

What it means is this: All humans inherit original sin from our first parents. But in the case of Mary alone, even though she was conceived naturally, that chain was broken. She didn't inherit original sin. She was conceived *immaculate,* which comes from a Latin word meaning "spotless." She didn't sin.

So remember: the Immaculate Conception refers to the conception of Mary in her mother's womb, not the conception of Jesus by Mary. That's where people on the Internet make their very common mistake.

At least this ignorance about the Immaculate Conception is nothing new. We can't say this is a big failure of our generation. Here's a note from a book from 1903: "It is remarkable how persistently people misunderstand the privilege of the Immaculate Conception. Dr. Haeckel, for instance, in his *Riddle of the Universe*, confounds it with 'the miraculous impregnation' of Mary, with which it has nothing to do."[10] If you've got a doctorate, Dr. Haeckel, you should know better! I don't actually know who Dr. Haeckel was, but apparently we haven't made much progress in teaching people about the Immaculate Conception in the last century or so.

*Side note*—if you're one of those who didn't know what the Immaculate Conception was when you first started reading this chapter, it's probably not your fault. Generations of Catholics have tragically missed out on the richness of Church teaching, and that's mostly because those who were supposed to be teaching these truths, well, didn't. Or they emphasized weird things that, at best, aren't good for us. Or they decided on their own that the things the Church had deemed good for us really weren't. Or they got lazy. Or, or, or. The weird thing is, it's probably not their fault either. This is what sin does: it passes falsehoods on until people decide to stop them—people like Archbishop Fulton Sheen, and St. Teresa of Calcutta, and St. John Paul II. They all put a stop to falsehoods in their own, unique ways. That's for another book, though. Getting back to Our Lady....

Why was Mary born without original sin? It was because God, who sees all eternity, had made His plan from the beginning of time, and that plan included one woman who would be God's own mother. Like the rest of the saints—including you and me, I hope—she was redeemed by the sacrifice of her Son, Jesus. But unlike the rest of us, she was redeemed from the moment of her conception. Why? Because her Son loved her, of course, and because it made her ready for the role she would have to take as the Mother of God.

Sometimes Protestants ask whether we worship Mary. (And sometimes they don't ask—they just state it as fact that we do worship Mary.) We don't, of course. *Worship* is for God alone. Mary is not God, nor do we think she's God. But we do *honor* her as the Mother of God. Why? Well, for one thing, Jesus told us to. When He was dying on the cross, He told his best friend John, "Behold your mother." That was meant for all of us. For another thing, Mary is naturally owed this honor. After all, she is the very mother of God! She is the woman God chose out of all the women on earth to take care of Him when he was a baby, to raise Him in a loving home, to be with Him when he started his ministry, and to wait with Him while he died on the cross.

I love it when people honor my mom. Jesus does, too, and Jesus and Mary both agree, I'm sure, that the best way to honor Mary is by following her good example of putting God above all. She wants to lead the way to holiness, but she can only lead if we're willing to follow. How can we follow? I think she's told us exactly what to do. If "do whatever he says" isn't enough, we have a much longer statement from Mother Mary to fill in the details.

## The Magnificat

Joseph is famous for not talking at all, or at least not when the Gospel writers could hear him. But we have a whole hymn composed by Mary in the Bible. This is what she gave us to guide us along the way to holiness. We call it the *Magnificat*, which is the first word in the Latin translation. To borrow a pop-psychology term that Mary might not have liked, we could call it her mantra. It was a summary of everything she believed about her relationship with God, and her relationship with God is the best model for our relationship with God. So the best way for us to find holiness is to follow her mantra—her Magnificat.

I use it as an examination of conscience. You know how, before you go to confession, you examine your conscience to see what's in there that you need to work on? Well, I don't know if there is a better examination of conscience for the Christian today than this. Mary's words here will lead us on the right path in our pursuit of holiness—which is the only reason we have life and liberty.

So we're going to go through the Magnificat line by line. I'll use the translation that many Catholics are familiar with from the liturgy, and we'll see how every line of Mary's hymn gives us something to think about—something to tell us where we are on the journey to holiness.

### *My soul Magnifies the Lord*

Stop right here.

Does *my* soul magnify the Lord? Can I say this first line with a clear conscience?

I'm not just talking about singing a song of praise. When the guitars come out of their cases, you can clap along with the best of them, I'm sure. But what's really in your soul? Do you just know the words and the tune, or are they expressing what really lives deep inside you? We're talking about the *soul* here, so we can't go any deeper than this.

This is what we have to ask ourselves: Is the Lord all I am about? Does everything that I do point back to Him in some way, shape or form?

Now, you may be thinking that's a tall order. When I go shopping for lumber at the home center, does that really have to point back to the Lord somehow? Am I supposed to be pointing back to the Lord when I order Chinese takeout? I don't even hesitate when I say yes. Yes, you are.

Think about it: what would Jesus do in your situation? Don't forget, Jesus was someone who worked with His hands. He knew what that was like. He knew what it was to go out and buy supplies, to deal with another small-business owner who had what He needed. So if He needed lumber, He'd get lumber, and somehow everyone

at the home center—or the first-century equivalent—
would be a little better off when He left. They might be
happier. They might be a little unsettled, however; for
the first time, they'd met someone who made them think
there was more to life than this, whatever this was.

Almost every life-changing encounter Jesus had was
with someone going about some kind of everyday business. He picked some of his disciples when they were in
their boats, fishing. He picked another one when he was
at the tax booth, checking boxes on forms. He met a Sa-
maritan woman who was doing typical women's work of
their day—drawing water from the well—and changed
her world. He changed not just her own life, but the lives
of the people around her, as she called all her friends to
come meet the man who seemed to know everything.

All these were everyday encounters in everyday sit-
uations, and yet they all changed lives. The place where
evangelizing happens is the everyday world, and it happens because your soul magnifies the Lord all the time.
Does that mean you have to shout "Praise the Lord!"
when you walk into the home center? No, of course not.
I think that would probably be counterproductive. People would hide from you, or at least they would suddenly
need plumbing supplies or whatever was way over there
at the other end of the store. No, the way to show God's
praises in everyday life is to imitate Christ, and Mary
did that.

So everywhere you go, get in the habit of remembering that people judge what a Christian is by what they see of you.

Which leads us straight into the next line.

### And my spirit rejoices in God my Savior

Are you a joyful Christian? Or are you a miserable Christian?

I know some people who act as though the whole Christian life is a big inconvenience to them. "Oh, I *have* to go to Mass. Oh, I'd *better* go to Confession. Oh, the parish festival is coming up, and I guess I *ought* to volunteer."

I get to visit a lot of parishes each year, speaking and giving parish missions. I meet and see a lot of people who serve the church in a variety of ways. Some serve on the parish council and others teach Sunday school. Some work in the Church office as the secretary or Director of Religious Formation. Others volunteer to bake the cakes and cookies for the parishioners to enjoy after that schmuck from Iowa is done speaking. Still others count the money after the collection, or run the respect life committee, or drive the donations each week to the local St. Vincent de Paul, or make sure Our Lord is being adored every hour by someone in the Perpetual Adoration Chapel. All that work is really important work. But sometimes, amidst all the people and things I see, there's something missing: *joy*. Yes, I'm amazed by the work they do. But without love, says St. Paul, we are just clashing symbols. When we love God, we serve Him. And we can't serve Him miserably. There's nothing more joyful than serving Him! Or, at least, there shouldn't be.

I can only imagine Mary as joyful. Why? Because she knew life was a gift, she was truly free (from sin), and she was holy. Who wouldn't be joyful with all three of those categories checked?

When I think of joyful Catholics, I always think of St. John Paul II. Every picture of him you see conveys the message that Christians have found the secret of happiness. But he wasn't always pope. When he was Karol Wojtyla, amidst all the suffering he endured at the hands of communism, people who knew him knew him as joyful, funny, light-hearted, and deeply in love with God.

Was his joy fake? No. He was filled with the Spirit, imitating Mary by rejoicing in God, his Savior. I think that's important for every Christian believer. We need to get in touch with that inner joy ourselves, and then we need to let everyone around us see it. That doesn't mean we have to be relentlessly cheerful all the time, but people should know that we have a source of joy—a joy that is born from our love for God.

*Because He has regarded the lowliness of His handmaid*

This is wildly ironic, isn't it? After all, Mary was created perfect! One might think she'd be tempted to brag that around, right? But she didn't, because that would be something someone who wasn't perfect would do. No, she understood that she was holy—but only because she was humble.

You've probably read about the Dunning-Kruger Effect. It's one of the Internet's favorite things to talk about—usually as an insult. The name comes from a study by David Dunning and Justin Kruger, who discovered, to summarize it badly, that people who know less about something tend to overestimate their own knowledge, whereas people who know more tend to *underestimate* their own knowledge. It's an interesting effect in psychology, but of course it's been appropriated by everyone who leaves comments on YouTube videos. Now "Dunning-Kruger" is one of the Internet's favorite insults to hurl at someone, implying that you're too stupid to know you're stupid. It seems that the less you know about the Dunning-Kruger Effect, the more you think you understand the Dunning-Kruger Effect. But the same effect works in the other direction, remember. We could put it this way: the more you know about something, the more humble you are, and the more you know about God, the more humble you are in the face of God.

There's a reason Christians consider humility a virtue, even though most of the rest of the world is fixated on "pride." It's because it takes humility to understand God's plan for you. Mary had a more important place in God's plan than anyone else since Adam and Eve.

Now, you and I don't know God nearly as well as his Mother does, but we can learn from Mary how to be humble. Yes, we have to be humble to be great. Without humility, we'll insist on following our way, not God's. And God will let us, because He's that kind of God. He gave us free will, remember. We can turn away from Him, and He'll let us. Oh, He'll run after us, plead with us, send us messages—but He won't make us come back. So we'll wander far away if we're too proud to listen to Him.

Therefore, we need to learn from Mary. If we imitate her humility, and really learn to think of ourselves as God's servants, then God will regard our lowliness, too. Then everyone will see that we have something special.


*For behold, henceforth all generations shall call me blessed*

Indeed we do, don't we? Blessed Virgin, Blessed Mother, Holy Mary, Full of Grace—we remember how blessed Mary is every time we mention her. But have you ever wondered why we call her the Blessed Mother? Well, here's the answer: "henceforth all generations shall call me blessed." It's right there in the Bible.

I get into arguments with my Protestant friends on this one, and I have to admit, I sometimes struggle to understand their position. You believe in "sola scriptura"—the Scriptures as your only guide to faith? Well, here it is! There's nothing more biblical than "henceforth all generations shall call me blessed." I can tell you the chapter and verse (Luke chapter 1, verse 48). There's nothing more biblical than calling her the Blessed Mother. She said it here!

But why was she so blessed? Because she was chosen to be God's mom. Yet, as we see, she doesn't make herself out to be anything special (though obviously she is). She already told us she was blessed because God "has regarded the lowliness of his handmaid." She emphasizes that again in the next line.

*Because He who is mighty has done great things for me, and holy is His name*

This is what real humility looks like. "My son is going to be the Messiah!" How could you keep from boasting about it? "Oh, *your* son the doctor, huh? Well, how about *my* son the Messiah?" But instead, she points out that God is the actor here. God has done great things for her; she hasn't done any great things by herself.

This shows us that Mary understood something better than any philosophical or theological giant—better than Paul, Augustine, Anselm, Aquinas, Catherine of Siena, or Teresa of Avila, as big as those names are in the history of thought. Mary understood gratitude. She was and is eternally thankful.

Are you a thankful person? I know I'm not thankful enough, but I try, and just the fact that I'm trying means that I'm doing better than I used to.

Gratitude is a simple thing until you start to think about it. Then you begin to realize that it's not natural at all. The natural state of things is that we want something, so we take it, now it's ours, and that's the end of the story. If you have children, how many times have you had to tell them to say "thank you" when somebody gives them something or does something for them? If you were ever a child (it's nothing to be ashamed of—a lot of us were), how many times did *your* parents have to tell you to say "thank you"?

Even when we've learned that lesson about the people around us, we still often forget to say "thank you" to God, who gives us literally everything. But I don't think you can have any kind of relationship with God without gratitude. You'll never get anywhere on the road to holiness until you've learned to say "thank you" properly. That's not because God *needs* our gratitude; it's because *we* need to be grateful. Until we learn gratitude, we haven't really got beyond the narrow little world of ourselves.

Gratitude leads us to praise God the right way—the way Mary does here, by remembering the amazing things He's done for her. That gives us the key to following in her footsteps: we have to remember the good things God has done for us. We have to remember them even when we're not all that happy with the way the world is going. The world may be broken by sin, but it's still very good, and we need to remember to thank God for that. The more things seem to be going badly for us (and Mary would have a lot of trouble in her life, too), the more grateful we need to be. How can we show that gratitude? Well, remembering this hymn by Mary is a good way to start!

### And His mercy is from generation to generation on those who fear Him

God didn't need to be merciful to Mary, right? She was conceived without sin. What does she know about God's mercy? I know God's mercy! I *need* God's mercy! But Mary . . . what did she need mercy for?

But that's the point. Mary knew God's mercy to the core of her being. She had experienced it firsthand in a way you and I can't even begin to imagine. Remember, Mary didn't create herself. She couldn't create herself; she's not God. But God shows his mercy to Mary in creating her the way He did. She knew that it was God's decision to show her that kind of favor; she'd had nothing to do with it.

That's what mercy is. It's God being good to us, not because we deserved it or made ourselves perfect, but because He loves us. "From generation to generation"—God's mercy never has an end for those who fear Him.

Now what does it mean to fear God? It doesn't mean to be afraid of Him, like He's some kind of monster. It means to be afraid of disappointing God, to be afraid of separating ourselves from God. In other words, the fear of God is the fear of sin, because sin is what separates us from God. So people who keep themselves from sin never lose God's mercy. Sinners also get God's mercy, of course—it's just that our sin will prevent us from accepting the mercy God is offering. To be in awe of God's mercy, and not to want to lose it—that's the kind of fear Mary is talking about.

Mary shows us what we can and *will* look like someday if we choose God's way over our own way. Remember, we have that liberty. But if we say, along with Mary, "May it be done to me according to your word," then we can be blessed the way she was blessed, all because of God's mercy. No wonder Mary was in awe of it! You can imagine her shaking her head and laughing in amazement at how incredible God really is and what He desires for the whole world.

*He has shown might with His arm;*

Ah! Here's where it gets really interesting! God's mercy wouldn't be worth anything to us if He didn't have the power to put it into action. But of course God has all the power in the world. That's what it means when we say God is *omnipotent*—it's just the Latin word for "all-powerful." The amazing thing is that God puts all that power at our service! There is literally nothing he won't do for our benefit, and that includes coming to earth in human form and dying on a cross.

Once again, Mary shows us how we should think about God and how we should praise God. She understood that God's power is not for God's benefit, but for the benefit of the creation He loves so much. When she thought about how He had put his strength to work for her, she was amazed.

So take Mary as your model, here. Think about how God has shown might with his arm, and remember to be grateful for it. What has God done for you? I don't know your whole biography, but I know how it starts: you were born. He gave you life! I'd say that's a pretty amazing beginning to the story, and Mary knew that the ending was going to be much more amazing than that. Meanwhile, she thought of all the other amazing things God had done for her and the rest of His people.

*He has scattered the proud in the conceit of their heart;*

Mary's on the side of God, not the side of the world. How do we know that? Because she was humble. But who are the proud? The proud are those who think they have it all figured out and they don't need God. Pride makes us think we know exactly how to sort out our lives and the world. It makes us want to be *mighty.* Spoiler alert: that never ends well, because . . .

*He has put down the mighty from their thrones,*

See, this is why you don't want to be mighty. Now, I'm sure some powerful people have only wanted to do good, and have only wanted to lead everyone to a better and holier life. I can't think of any at the moment, but I'm sure they've existed. But the thing about being rich and powerful is that it makes your job really hard. Remember that your real job is to be a saint. Pursuing holiness is a full-time occupation.

In my book *Your God Is Too Boring,* I mentioned that if you see the world as a Christian, you have to see the world upside-down. Everything the world tells you will make you happy . . . doesn't. God knows that. So all the power and money the world tells you that you want? Those things just lead to misery if not put in their proper place.

There's a reason the pope calls himself the Servant of the Servants of God. He knows that popes get in trouble when they start to think of themselves as big and important. These days, the pope may be the most powerful person on the planet, but it's a strange kind of power. It only exists if he's completely humble and dedicated, because his power is moral power. He can *persuade* a billion Catholics to be better people, but as soon as he tries to *make* anybody do something, his power is gone. It was different in the old days, when the popes were kings, too, with a large territory in central Italy and an army that often got into fights with their neighbors. Do you know what God did about that? He put them down from their throne—the secular throne, that is. So you don't want to be high and mighty in your heart. You want to be humble. Because....

*and has exalted the lowly.*

When Jesus was invited to dinner with a well-known Pharisee, He had some advice for the guests:

> When you are invited by someone to a wedding banquet, do not recline at table in the place of honor. A more distinguished guest than you may have been invited by him, and the host who

invited both of you may approach you and say, 'Give your place to this man,' and then you would proceed with embarrassment to take the lowest place. Rather, when you are invited, go and take the lowest place so that when the host comes to you he may say, 'My friend, move up to a higher position.' Then you will enjoy the esteem of your companions at the table. For everyone who exalts himself will be humbled, but the one who humbles himself will be exalted. (Luke 14:8–11)

This is the way it always is with God. Who was the greatest king in Israel's history? David. Who was he? Nobody! He was a shepherd boy, the last and least of all Jesse's sons. He was so unimportant that when Samuel the prophet showed up and *specifically asked* to meet Jesse's sons, Jesse didn't even bother to call David. That was the lowly man God chose to exalt.

Who are God's people? The poor. Over and over again we see this in Sacred Scripture. Remember the rich young man who didn't want to sell all he had when Jesus asked him to (see Luke 18:22–23). His riches were getting in his way.

That story makes you nervous, doesn't it? "But Jon," you say, "I'm not poor! I have two cars, a nice home, and a comfy chair. Am I that rich young man?" Well, I'm rich, too. You and I are the one percent, remember? Or maybe the two percent. If we're living above the poverty line in America, most of the world looks at us with envy.

Yes, God does love the materially poor. After all, He came to us without material riches. He grew up in a family that was, at best, lower middle class. He had to work with His hands to scrape by. I guess that shows us who His favorites are. But He seeks another kind of poverty, and that's the poverty of the heart. Remember the very beginning of the Sermon on the Mount: "Blessed are the poor in spirit, for theirs is the kingdom of Heaven" (Matthew 5:3). He doesn't just say, "Blessed are the poor." He says, "Blessed are the poor *in spirit*." He means people who are humble. He means people like Mary, who are willing to say, "Let it be done to me according to your word."

### He has filled the hungry with good things

Oh! A great big plate of fettuccine Alfredo, and some garlic bread, and tiramisu for dessert, please! Wait, that's not what she means?

Well, no. It's not that God doesn't care about the physically hungry, but remember the Sermon on the Mount again: "Blessed are they who hunger and thirst for righteousness, for they will be satisfied" (Matthew 5:6). It's not "Blessed are they who hunger for pasta smothered in cream and Parmesan and thirst for a good Chianti." Jesus isn't *guaranteeing* that you'll get those things. But He does guarantee that you'll get what you want if you hunger and thirst for righteousness.

Does your soul hunger for God? Mary's did. She was always looking to fill herself with the good things of God. Often, we're trying to fill ourselves with something else. Usually, it's not as simple as Italian food—although it could be, if food becomes an obsession. Food does become an obsession all too often in our society. Some people like food way too much (not that I know anyone like that). Also, some people constantly consume themselves with the details of their nutrition, until, as St. Paul says, "Their God is their stomach" (Philippians 3:19). Food is good, and taking care of our health is a good thing, too. But if you put it before everything else, our god isn't God anymore.

When our soul hungers for God, it means that God is the most important thing in our life. This is where we really need to build up that relationship with God, the way the saints we talked about earlier did. Remember that we are made in the image of God so that we *can* have a relationship with him. The better we know Him, the more we'll want to know God even better. That's the hunger Mary and Jesus both talked about—the hunger to be closer and closer to God.

*and the rich He has sent away empty.*

Hasn't Mary been clear enough yet about the kind of heart God desires? Well, here she makes the choice explicit. Namely, we either go to God empty and be filled, or we go to God filled and leave empty. Of course that's good news for the people who are empty, but it sounds like bad news for the people who are filled. In the end, anything we're filled with other than God is in our way. We're pursuing holiness. If deep down there's something in you that thinks you're so special that you can get along without God, it's good to give that over to God.

*He has given help to Israel, his servant,*
*mindful of His mercy*

This is the Church that Mary is talking about here. We are the descendants of Abraham, the children of the promise (see Romans 5:7). That makes us, the people of the Church, Israel—the people of God, and the Church is here to serve God. This is who we are and why we're here. In the service of the gospel is the only way to live. But we can't do it by ourselves, can we? Very fortunately, we don't have to do it by ourselves. "And behold, I am with you always, until the end of the age," Jesus said when He sent His disciples out to all nations. The end of the age hasn't happened yet. Jesus is still with His Church. He's still sending the Holy Spirit to give His Church the power to proclaim the Gospel, and to do it *without error.*

That certainly doesn't mean that individual Catholics can't be wrong. Even the pope can be wrong unless he's speaking on a matter of faith or morals, and even then he has to be speaking *as pope*, not just as some guy who lives in the Vatican. But when the pope is speaking for the Church in matters of faith and morals, the Holy Spirit protects him from teaching wrong doctrine. The Spirit does that because the whole Church is protected from teaching wrong doctrine. Mary, as the Mother of the Church, knows better than anybody how much God loves His Church. He never forgets His mercy.

*Even as he spoke to our fathers, to Abraham and to his posterity forever.*

God wins in the end, and Mary knows this. Abraham was the great founder of the faith in one God, and it was to Abraham that God made the spectacular promise that his descendants would be as numerous as the stars of Heaven. Actually, He made that promise *three times* (see Genesis 15:5, 22:17, 26:4).

I don't think most of us realize what that means. These days, most people live in the city or the suburbs, and you look up and see a couple of dozen stars on a good night. Big deal. Abraham is going to have, what, twenty-five descendants?

Go out into the country sometime and look at the stars. Star-gazing clubs in most big cities would be happy to tell you the next time they're going out to gaze, and they know where the good spots are—the spots where the sky is unobstructed and the lights aren't too bright to see anything. If you're out in the really dark countryside, suddenly you know what God meant when He made that promise. Suddenly you see why our ancestors lived in awe of the night sky. Astronomers estimate that you can actually distinguish four or five thousand stars in the night sky with your unaided eye, but the Milky Way—which you never see in the city—adds the light of approximately a gazillion more (*gazillion* is a technical astronomical term) that you can't pick out individually.

That's us. Somewhere in those gazillion stars, you can imagine you and me, two of the gazillions of descendants God promised Abraham. We're the descendants of Abraham. We're the Church, and God is always faithful to his people. This is what He promises us first! God is faithful to us.

So now it's our turn. We give ourselves over to Him. That's gratitude, which I seem to remember we talked about before.

## Mary Shows Us How to Be Grateful

Gratitude is one of the most important facets of our spiritual life, because it reminds us that we depend on God completely. We can't do it by ourselves; we can't walk that road to holiness without constant inputs from God's grace. In fact, that's one of the most important teachings of the Church. Like many other important teachings, it had to be defined for the first time when somebody said it wasn't true. In this case, it was somebody named Pelagius, who said that human beings could attain Heaven under their own steam, just by making the right choices. St. Augustine wrote the most important arguments against "Pelagianism."

It's a delicate balance, like most Church doctrines. There's a straight and narrow path of truth between the extremes of falsehood. "How narrow the gate and constricted the road that leads to life" (Matthew 7:14), as Jesus himself said. On the one hand, the Pelagian heresy imagined that we could do everything by our own choices. On the other hand, some Christians (like traditional Calvinists) deny that we have free will at all. If you really believe that, you'll just sit back and not try. Maybe you're among the elect, maybe you're not. Not your job.

Fortunately, we have Mary to show us the right way. What have we learned from her?

The Lord should be all we're about—even in everyday life.

We need to be joyful, even if it takes some work at first.

We also need to be humble, so that we'll follow God's way and not our own.

We should never forget to call Mary blessed—because she's showing us the way to the same blessings.

We should remember to be grateful the way Mary is always grateful.

We fear God the right way when the worst thing we can imagine is being separated from God.

God puts his power at our service.

Pride—thinking we can do without God—leads to terrible sin . . .

. . . but God will send us a cure for our pride.

The poor in spirit are blessed because they'll let God do things His way.

The people who are full of themselves may need some emptying out first.

God will always keep His Church protected.

Then we, the descendants of Abraham, give ourselves back to God.

Chief among all we learn is understanding that all of the above is God's work, not ours. We just have to, as St. Teresa of Calcutta said, "Give God permission."

So, there you are. Every time the Magnificat comes up in church, or every time you read it in Luke's Gospel, or every time you pray it at home, you can remember that in Mary we find the blueprint to right relationship with God.

## On Our Way

We're always on our way somewhere. After I finish a few paragraphs here, I'll be on my way to dinner. Then I'll be on my way to bed. Tomorrow morning, you may be on your way to work, or on your way to church, or on your way to the dentist.

But none of those places is your ultimate destination. We only have two ultimate destinations: you can be with God and be happy forever, or you can choose to go the other way, because you think it will make you happy. I think you know by now that it won't. But you do have the freedom to make that choice, because God made you with liberty. In the abstract, it doesn't sound like a hard choice. Do you want to go to Heaven or Hell? One ticket for Heaven, please. I looked up Hell online, and it got, like, one-star reviews. Easy decision, right? Well, if that were the way the decision appeared to us all the time, we wouldn't have any trouble with all this freedom we've got. Satan would have to close up shop, and no one would come to the going-out-of-business sale. That's why Satan has to be clever. Each little individual decision we make is part of that big decision: Heaven or Hell? But Satan doesn't want us to see that. He wants us to think in the short term, like the five year old who wants the cookie. He wants us to look at the trees and miss the forest, just like we did in Eden.

So what do we do to outwit Satan? I think we go the other direction. If Satan is going to be clever, we'll be simple. If he's going to mire us in details, we're going to stick with the big picture. Like St. Joseph, we're going to be quiet and listen to God. Like Brother Lawrence, we'll be happy just to know that God is with us and that we can have a conversation with Him the way we do with our best friends. Like St. Teresa, we're going to keep pushing inward through the rooms in that interior castle until we meet God at the center of our being. And like Mother Mary, we'll be grateful all our lives for the things God has given us, for all the wonderful fruits in the garden that we can have.

It's going to mean giving some things up. We'll have to lose our attachment to all those things that the world around us wants us to think make life worthwhile. Instead, we'll follow Mother Mary. We'll be humble and joyful— even if we don't always feel joyful. We'll trust God to show might with his arm. We'll hunger and thirst for righteousness, and we'll know that God will fill us with good things.

God gave us liberty, and we're going to get death sooner or later. But death is just the beginning of eternity for us. We're going to use our liberty to make the right choices, and we're going to trust God to give us the grace to make those choices when they come to us. We're not going after the shiny baubles of this life. We're pursuing holiness.

**FOR REFLECTION**

I can only imagine Mary as joyful. Why? Because she knew life was a gift.

*What is one way I can strengthen my devotion to Mother Mary?*

# Notes

1. Health Resources and Services Administration, "The 'Loneliness Epidemic'" (https://www.hrsa.gov/enews/past-issues/2019/january-17/loneliness-epidemic).

2. "Self-Reported Life Satisfaction," Our World in Data (https://ourworld-indata.org/happiness-and-life-satisfaction).

3. Homily of His Holiness John Paul II, Oriole Park at Camden Yards, Baltimore, Sunday, 8 October 1995

4. The Way of Perfection, p. 2.

5. The Way of Perfection, pp. 8-9.

6. Foundations, pp. 2-3.

7. Pope John Paul II: 8th World Youth Day, Eucharistic Celebration at the Cherry Creek State Park of Denver, Homily Of His Holiness John Paul II (http://www.vatican.va/content/john-paul-ii/en/homilies/1993/documents/hf_jp-ii_hom_19930815_gmg-denver.html).

8. Lydia Saad, "Catholics' Church Attendance Resumes Downward Slide," Gallup News, April 9, 2019 (https://news.gallup.com/poll/232226/church-attendance-among-catholics-resumes-downward-slide.aspx); "In U.S., Decline of Christianity Continues at Rapid Pace," Pew Research Center, October 17, 2019 (https://www.pewforum.org/2019/10/17/in-u-s-decline-of-christianity-continues-at-rapid-pace/)

9. Matthew Gambino, "Half of Catholics attending Mass 28 years ago no longer do, figures show," CatholicPhilly.com, September 5, 2019 (https://catholicphilly.com/2019/09/our-changing-church/half-of-catholics-attending-mass-28-years-ago-no-longer-do-figures-show-2/)

10. Joseph McCabe: Church Discipline: An Ethical Study of the Church of Rome, p. 141.

# Bibliography

G. K. Chesterton: *Orthodoxy*. New York and London: John Lane, 1908.

Matthew Gambino, "Half of Catholics attending Mass 28 years ago no longer do, figures show," CatholicPhilly.com, September 5, 2019 (https://catholicphilly.com/2019/09/our-changing-church/half-of-catholics-attending-mass-28-years-ago-no-longer-do-figures-show-2/)

Health Resources and Services Administration, "The 'Loneliness Epidemic'" (https://www.hrsa.gov/enews/past-issues/2019/january-17/loneliness-epidemic)

Brother Lawrence of the Resurrection: *Maximes spirituelles fort utiles aux âmes pieuses, pour acquérir la présence de Dieu*. Paris: Edme Couterot, 1691.

Brother Lawrence of the Resurrection: *La Théologie de la présence de Dieu*. Cologne: Jean de la Pierre, 1710.

Brother Lawrence of the Resurrection: *The Practice of the Presence of God*. New York and London: Fleming H. Revell Company, 1895.

St. John Paul II: *Homily of His Holiness John Paul II*, Oriole Park at Camden Yards, Baltimore, Sunday, 8 October 1995 (http://www. vatican.va/content/john-paul-ii/en/homilies/1995/documents/ hf_jp-ii_hom_19951008_baltimore.html).

St. John Paul II: *Homily Of His Holiness John Paul II*, 8th World Youth Day, Eucharistic Celebration at the Cherry Creek State Park of Denver, Sunday, 15 August 1993 (http://www.vatican. va/content/john-paul-ii/en/homilies/1993/documents/hf_jp-ii_ hom_19930815_gmg-denver.html).

Joseph McCabe: *Church Discipline: An Ethical Study of the Church of Rome*. London: Duckworth & Co., 1903.

Lydia Saad, "Catholics' Church Attendance Resumes Downward Slide," Gallup News, April 9, 2019 (https://news.gallup.com/ poll/232226/church-attendance-among-catholics-resumes-downward-slide.aspx)

St. Teresa of Jesus (Teresa of Avila): *The Interior Castle*. Translated by the Benedictines of Stanbrook, with introduction by Benedict Zimmerman. New York, Cincinnati, Chicago: Benziger Brothers, 1906.

St. Teresa of Jesus (Teresa of Avila): *The Way of Perfection*. Edited by A. R. Waller. London: J. M. Dent & Co., 1902.

St. Teresa of Jesus (Teresa of Avila): *Book of the Foundations*. Translated from the Spanish by the Rev. John Dalton. London: T. Jones, 1853.

Anonymous, "Self-Reported Life Satisfaction," Our World in Data (https://ourworldindata.org/happiness-and-life-satisfaction)

Anonymous, "In U.S., Decline of Christianity Continues at Rapid Pace," Pew Research Center, October 17, 2019

## About the Author

JON LEONETTI IS A NATIONALLY KNOWN CATHOLIC speaker, best-selling author, and radio host who conveys a message of lasting fulfillment in Jesus Christ. Through Jon's keynote presentations and parish missions, thousands of Catholics each year discover the freedom Christ offers by way of his life and love.

Jon is the founder of SanctifyU, a first of its kind membership platform on the lives, teachings, and wisdom of the saints, and the author of three other books: *Mission of the Family*, *Your God Is too Boring*, and *The Art of Getting Over Yourself: And Why You'll Be Happier When You Do*.

Jon believes that our deepest longing for happiness and wholeness is fulfilled in the encounter with Jesus Christ. Through prayer, the Sacraments, family life, and the help of Mary and the saints, Jon wants to cultivate an intimate relationship with Jesus, and help others do the same.

# SURGE OF THE HEART

*Three Evenings—One Mission—Totally Catholic*

*Engaging presentations.*
*Inspiring Stories.*
*A call to conversion.*

"One of the most inspiring parish missions
available in America today."

MATTHEW KELLY
Founder of Dynamic Catholic

Learn more at
www.JonLeonetti.com

**NOTES**

**NOTES**